iBoo Press House uses state-of-the-art technology to digitally reconstruct the work. We preserve the original format whilst repairing imperfections present in the aged copy.

All Deluxe Edition titles are unabridged designed with a nice Digital Cloth™ Blue Cover underneath the dusk jacket, quality paper and a large font that's easy to read.

visit iBoo.com to see our all DELUXE EDITIONS.

iBoo

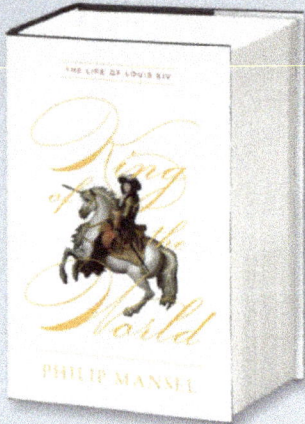

King of the World
The Life of Louis XIV
Philip Mansel

"Copiously, beautifully, and intelligently illustrated, complemented by excellent maps and diagrams (notably a ground-plan of Versailles), *King of the World* is one of the most stimulating and enjoyable works on European history to have been published for many a long year."
—*Wall Street Journal*
Cloth $35.00

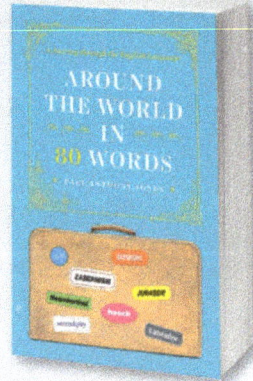

Around the World in 80 Words
A Journey through the English Language
Paul Anthony Jones

"A fabulous and erudite survey of words inspired by place names.... Logophiles will have a ball."
—*Publishers Weekly*, starred review
Paper $18.00

Mental Traveler
A Father, a Son, and a Journey through Schizophrenia
W. J. T. Mitchell

"A kaleidoscopic and erudite memoir of madness and sanity, this is also, at its core, a stunning account of what endures in the wake of catastrophic tragedies: love, art, and vast stores of human hope."—Rachel DeWoskin, author of *Banshee* and *Two Menus*
Cloth $22.50

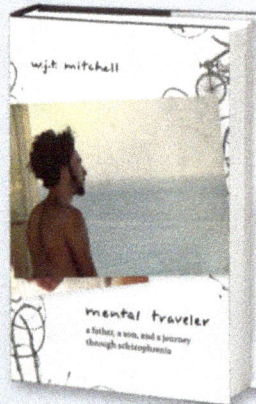

A History of the Second World War in 100 Maps
Jeremy Black

In this thrilling book, Jeremy Black blends his singular cartographic and military expertise into a captivating overview of World War II from the air, sea, and sky, making clear how fundamental maps were to every aspect of the global conflict.
Cloth $35.00

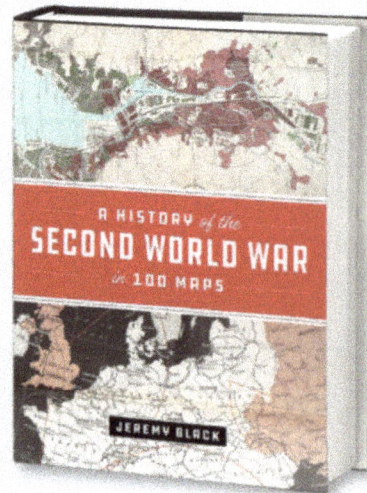

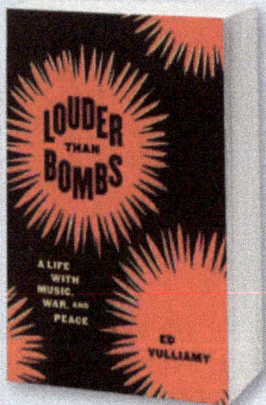

Louder Than Bombs
A Life with Music, War, and Peace
Ed Vulliamy

"An impressively rich affair.... [*Louder than Bombs*] is not only a testament to a life-long love of music, it also represents an indefatigable act of reportage into it."—*Financial Times*
Paper $20.00

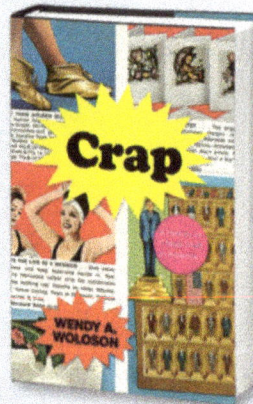

Crap
A History of Cheap Stuff in America
Wendy A. Woloson

"The book is sympathetic to our impulse toward crap, if not toward crap itself or its production. ...*Crap* is insightful in its analyses of the way cheap stuff has worked to appease our aspirations."—*Baffler*
Cloth $29.99

Two collections from David Tracy

"There are not many authors who share both the breadth of vision and depth of reading and scholarship that Tracy has."—John McCarthy, Loyola University Chicago

Volume 1
Fragments
The Existential Situation of Our Time: Selected Essays
Cloth $39.00

Volume 2
Filaments
Theological Profiles: Selected Essays
Cloth $39.00

Shoddy
From Devil's Dust to the Renaissance of Rags
Hanna Rose Shell

"The fascinating story of how a respectable textile product became synonymous with all things inferior.... [Shell] writes with an eye for both vivid visuals and historical links.... It's a fun ride."
—*Washington Independent Review of Books*
Cloth $25.00

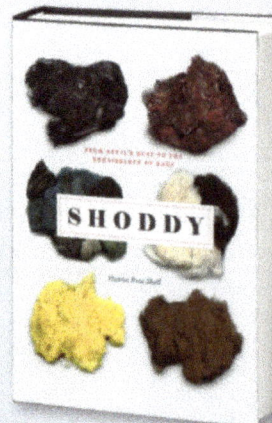

Your shopping list starts here...

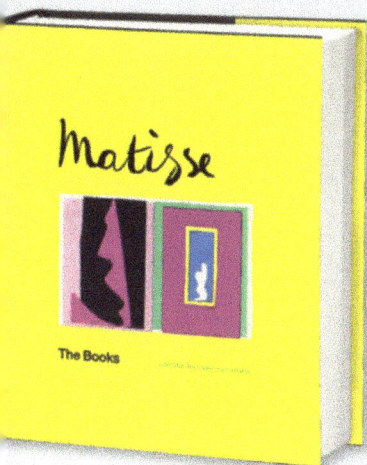

Matisse
The Books
Louise Rogers Lalaurie

"[A] fresh, in-depth, lavishly illustrated study."—*Financial Times*

"These books-as-works-of-art are both a running commentary upon Matisse himself, the ever evolving, ever surprising image-maker, and an extraordinarily vivid series of critical responses to words that are often so rich and elusive in their meanings."—*Hyperallergic*

Cloth $75.00

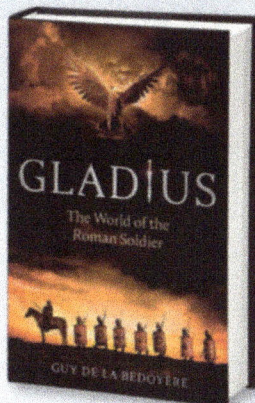

Gladius
The World of the Roman Soldier
Guy de la Bédoyère

"A highly successful introduction to the life of the Roman soldier. Making use of a wide range of sources, de la Bédoyère's informative and readable book offers real immediacy to readers."—Clifford Ando, University of Chicago

Cloth $30.00

Leave Me Alone and I'll Make You Rich
How the Bourgeois Deal Enriched the World
Deirdre Nansen McCloskey and Art Carden

Read this book and learn why you must know the truth, what truth you need to know, and why the freedom it brings has made almost everyone better off than their parents and grandparents."— Vernon L. Smith, Chapman University and 2002 Nobel Laureate in Economics

Cloth $25.00

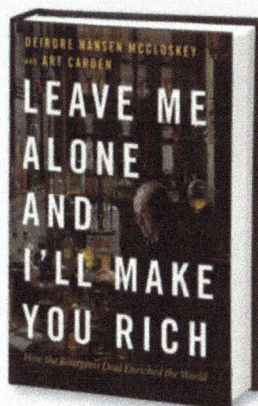

Strata
William Smith's Geological Maps
Edited by the Oxford University Museum of Natural History
With an Introduction by Douglas Palmer and with a Foreword by Robert Macfarlane

"William Smith was a terranaut—a deep-time visionary who taught himself to see down into bedrock and crust. . . His map exists somewhere between artwork, dreamwork, and data-set."—Robert Macfarlane, from the foreword

Cloth $65.00

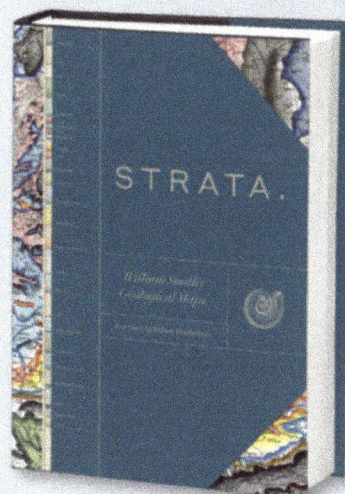

The Pocket Stoic
John Sellars

"Sellars's book is an excellent starting point for anyone interested in experimenting with this approach to life."—*Five Books*

Cloth $12.00

The Eighth
Mahler and the World in 1910
Stephen Johnson

"[A] thrilling study of Gustav Mahler's Symphony No 8. . . . Johnson makes a strong case for its quality, musically and philosophically, in this magnificent, strongly argued, and yet wonderfully subtle study."—John Banville, *Guardian*

Cloth $26.00

Land's End
New and Selected Poems
Gail Mazur

"Here, as elsewhere, Mazur boldly and sensitively proclaims her own lack of understanding. It is this vulnerability, equipped and complemented with extensive erudition, that makes Mazur's poems as poignant as they are accomplished in their craft."—*Publishers Weekly,* starred review

Phoenix Poets

Cloth $25.00

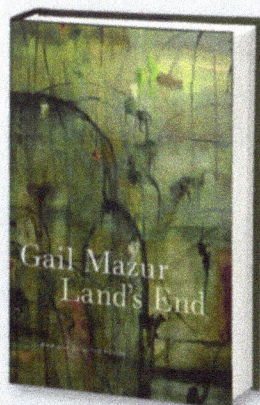

Hooked
Art and Attachment
Rita Felski

"*Hooked* is a marvelous achievement. It is a rousing book that returns to one of the main questions at the heart of Felski's scholarship—how people become attached to particular works of literature or art."—James English, University of Pennsylvania

Paper $22.50

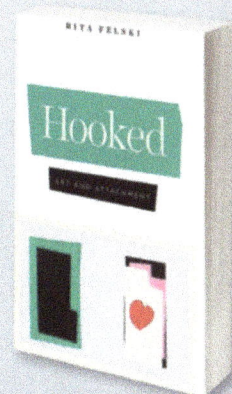

The University of Chicago Press   www.press.uchicago.edu

Bisa Butler

NOW OPEN

Portraits

ART
INSTITVTE
CHICAGO

Catalogue available at publications.artic.edu

Bisa Butler: Portraits is co-organized by the Art Institute of Chicago the Katonah Museum of Art.

Corporate Sponsor

Major funding for *Bisa Butler: Portraits* is contributed by the Cav Family Trust. Additional support is provided by The Joyce Found: and Darrel and Nickol Hackett. Bisa Butler, *Broom Jumpers* (de 2019. Mount Holyoke College Art Museum, Purchase with the Bell Hy Baier Art Acquisition Fund. ©Bisa Butler. Photo by Margaret Fe

Allstate
You're in good hands.

The Reader's House

Published by Newyox

LONDON OFFICE
3rd Floor
86-90 Paul Street
London
EC2A 4NE UK

t: +44 20 3828 7097
editor@newyox.com
www.newyox.com

For all advertising and promotional opportunities contact at editor@newyox.com

CONTRIBUTORS

Andy Machin
By Abby Abhinav
Lisa Brown Gilbert
Savvy Intrapreneur
Razan Azzarkani
Josh Hoxie

We assume no responsibility for unsolicited manuscripts or art materials.

NEW & NOTABLE

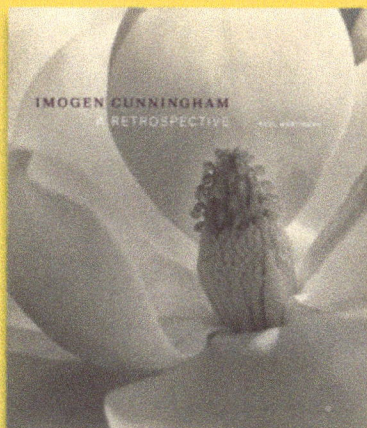

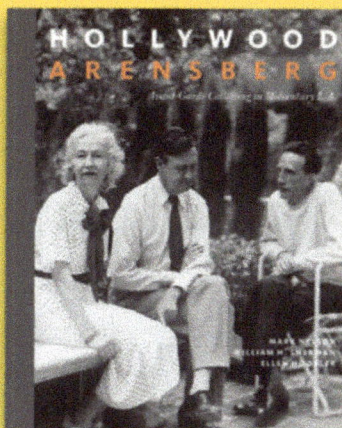

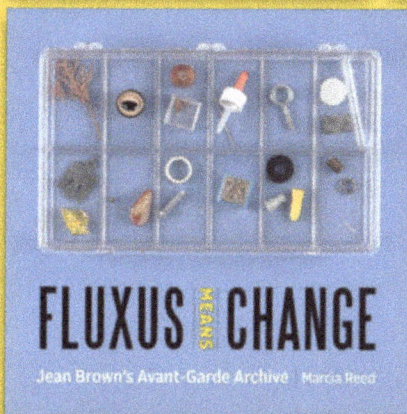

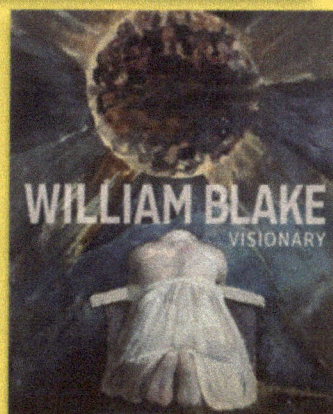

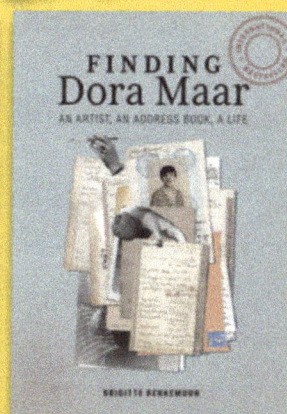

Imogen Cunningham
A Retrospective
Paul Martineau

Thoroughly researched and beautifully produced, this book offers a comprehensive look at the motivations and extraordinary work of the American photographer.

Fluxus Means Change
Jean Brown's Avant-Garde Archive
Marcia Reed

An exploration of the radical artists who transformed the ways art is conceived, exhibited, and collected, through the Dada, Surrealist, and Fluxus collections of Jean and Leonard Brown.

Hollywood Arensberg
Avant-Garde Collecting in Midcentury L.A.
Mark Nelson, William H. Sherman, and Ellen Hoobler

"Beyond being an awe-inspiring dive into the art holdings of the Arensbergs, the book offers a complex portrait of two people working to shape multiple fields."

—Andrew Russeth,
Architectural Digest

William Blake
Visionary
Edina Adam and Julian Brooks, with an essay by Matthew Hargraves

A richly illustrated, comprehensive introduction to the British artist who continues to inspire musicians, poets, performers, and visual artists worldwide.

Mira Calligraphiae Monumenta
A Sixteenth-Century Calligraphic Manuscript Inscribed by Georg Bocskay and Illuminated by Joris Hoefnagel
2ND EDITION

Lee Hendrix and Thea Vignau-Wilberg

A treasury of extraordinary beauty to inspire book lovers, graphic designers, and scholars alike.

Finding Dora Maar
An Artist, an Address Book, a Life
Brigitte Benkemoun

Translated by Jody Gladding

"[A] spirited and deeply researched project.... [Benkemoun's] affection for her subject is infectious. This book gives a satisfying treatment to a woman who has been confined for decades to a Cubist's limited interpretation."

—Joumana Khatib,
The New York Times

When we feel stressed our nervous system pushes signals to the brain that things are not quite right. It senses danger or a threat.

The Basics of Understanding Stress

By Andy Machin

Stress comes to us all in different ways at different times in different degrees and any number of causes can trigger it. When stressed we feel that we care not in control. We feel overwhelmed.

When that happens, something needs to be done about it. You must do what you can to manage your stress and regain control. But just what is stress? That's what we look at here so you may understand what stress is and how we react to it.

When we feel stressed our nervous system pushes signals to the brain that things are not quite right. It senses danger or a threat. The brain then reacts - often known as "fight or flight" - and hormones go crazy often causing the classic stress symptoms of increased heart rate, faster breathing (gasping for breath), increased blood pressure and more.

Basically this is how the body automatically reacts to anything causing you to feel stressed. It's a signal to do something about it. Unless you do, the stress can spiral and quickly get more serious in turn affecting your health - you may well end up depressed or feeling down for example. And that's never good.

Now we have a basic understanding of what stress is, let's take a look at some of the ways we respond when stressed.

We mostly feel on edge, uncomfortable, perhaps even desperate if the stress is particularly bad. You may feel emotional, frustrated and irritable too because you do not know how to get things back in order again.

This can spill over in to your relationships - partner, family, friends, and colleagues - as they will pick up on how you are feeling and that could affect them in different ways too. Some may offer help, some might simply keep out of your way.

Some people respond to stress by withdrawing in to themselves and distancing themselves from others in an attempt to cope. This can often make things worse and the stress and whatever is causing it remains bottled up inside you. Whereas talking things out with a close friend often is a huge help. A problem shared is a problem halves as the saying goes.

Some people respond to stress by withdrawing in to themselves and distancing themselves from others in an attempt to cope. This can often make things worse and the stress and whatever is causing it remains bottled up inside you. Whereas talking things out with a close friend often is a huge help. A problem shared is a problem halves as the saying goes.

Some people may appear to be cool, calm and collected when stressed in an attempt to hide it. A bit like a duck in water. The duck looks serene going about its business, but underneath it's paddling away. So it may be with a person who reacts to stress by trying to hide it.

The story here is that by having and understanding of what stress is, what causes it and how we react to it differently may help you to deal with it next time you feel stressed and take action to reduce your stress.

Source: EzineArticles

FIELDING
HENRY

FIELDING

Henry Fielding (22 April 1707 – 8 October 1754) was an English novelist and dramatist known for his earthy humour and satire, and as the author of the comic novel Tom Jones. He also holds a place in the history of law enforcement, having used his authority as a magistrate to found the Bow Street Runners, which some have called London's first police force.

Fielding was born at Sharpham, Somerset, and educated at Eton College, where he established a lifelong friendship with William Pitt the Elder. His mother died when he was 11. A suit for custody was brought by his grandmother against his charming but irresponsible father, Lt Gen. Edmund Fielding. The settlement placed Henry in his grandmother's care, although he continued to see his father in London. In 1725, Henry tried to abduct his cousin, Sarah Andrews, while she was on her way to church. He fled to avoid prosecution. In 1728, he travelled to Leiden to study classics and law at the university. However, lack of money obliged him to return to London and he began writing for the theatre. Some of his work was savagely critical of the government of Prime Minister Sir Robert Walpole. Dramatist and novelist The Theatrical Licensing Act of 1737 is said to be a direct response to his activities in writing for the theatre. Although the play that triggered the act was the unproduced, anonymously authored The Golden Rump, Fielding's dramatic satires had set the tone. Once it was passed, political satire on the stage became virtually impossible. Fielding retired from the theatre and resumed his career in law to support his wife Charlotte Craddock and two children by becoming a barrister.

Fielding's lack of financial acumen meant he and his family often endured periods of poverty, but he was helped by Ralph Allen, a wealthy benefactor, on whom Squire Allworthy in Tom Jones would be based. Allen went on to provide for the education and support of Fielding's children after the writer's death.

Henry Fielding, about 1743, etching by Jonathan Wild Fielding never stopped writing political satire and satires of current arts and letters. The Tragedy of Tragedies (for which Hogarth designed the frontispiece) was, for example, quite successful as a printed play. Based on his earlier Tom Thumb, this was another of Fielding's "irregular" plays published under the name of H. Scriblerus Secundus, a pseudonym

intended to link himself ideally with the Scriblerus Club of literary satirists founded by Jonathan Swift, Alexander Pope and John Gay. He also contributed a number of works to journals of the time.

From 1734 until 1739 he wrote anonymously for the leading Tory periodical, The Craftsman, against the Prime Minister, Sir Robert Walpole. Fielding's patron was the opposition Whig MP George Lyttelton, a boyhood friend from Eton. Lyttelton followed his leader Lord Cobham in forming a Whig opposition to Walpole's government called the Cobhamites (which included another of Fielding's Eton friends, William Pitt). In the Craftsman, Fielding voiced the opposition attack on bribery and corruption in British politics. Although writing for the opposition to Walpole, which included Tories as well as Whigs, Fielding was "unshakably a Whig" and often praised Whig heroes such as the Duke of Marlborough and Gilbert Burnet.

Fielding dedicated his play Don Quixote in England to the opposition Whig leader Lord Chesterfield. It was published on 17 April 1734, the same day writs were issued for the general election. He dedicated his 1735 play The Universal Gallant to Charles Spencer, 3rd Duke of Marlborough, a political follower of Chesterfield. The other prominent opposition newspaper, Common Sense, founded by Chesterfield and Lyttelton, was named after a character in Fielding's Pasquin (1736). Fielding wrote at least two articles for it in 1737 and 1738.

Fielding continued to air his political views in satirical articles and newspapers in the late 1730s and early 1740s. He was the main writer and editor from 1739 to 1740 for the satirical paper The Champion, which was heavily critical of Walpole's government and of pro-government literary and political writers. He sought to avoid charges of libel by making its political attacks so funny or embarrassing to the victim that a publicized court case would seem even worse. He later became chief writer for the Whig government of Henry Pelham.

Fielding took to novel writing in 1741, angered by Samuel Richardson's success with Pamela; or, Virtue Rewarded. His first success was an anonymous parody of that: Shamela. This follows the model of Tory satirists of the previous generation, notably Swift and Gay.

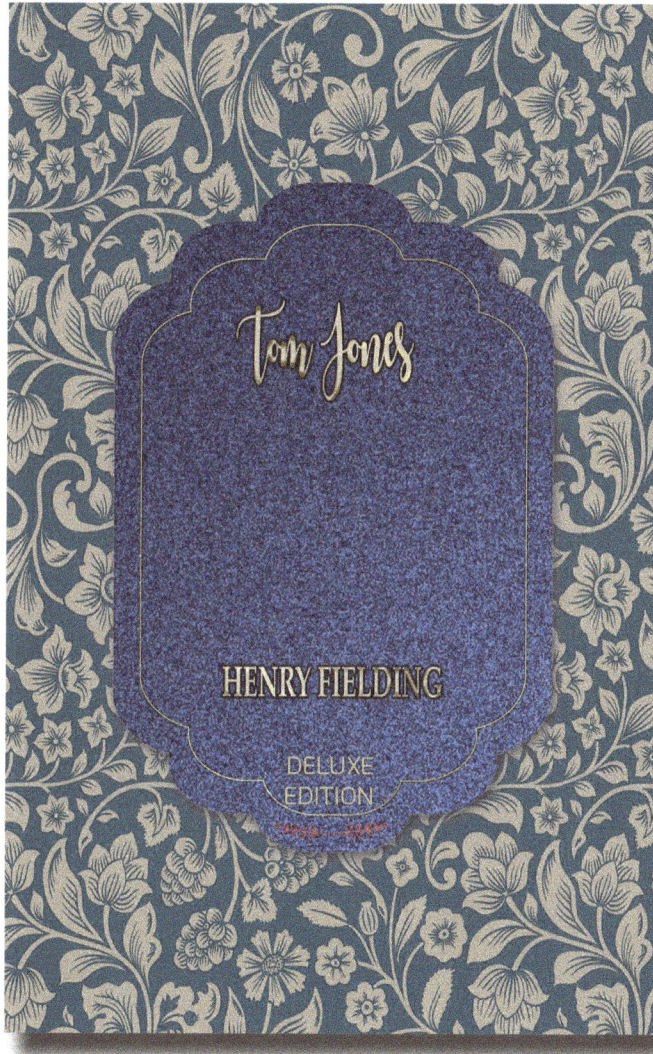

How to Sell EBooks on Amazon

There is a lot to know about "how to sell an eBook on different platforms" however we would be talking about the most popular platform right now and that is Amazon.

By Abby Abhinav

It's better to know why to sell an eBook before knowing how to sell. As everything is getting online then why not selling and buying of an item? Yes, you got that right. We are now in next-gen where selling an item is not as difficult as compared to the old time wherein everything was sold out manually by approaching a person or a company or distributing it offline through different showrooms or shops.

Writing a Book is a hectic job and must be paid out accordingly. Authors and publishers used to spend a lot on getting their content printed, published as well as marketed. Sending books to different bookshelves and popular libraries so that their writings could be sold out and they get the monetary return at the earliest possible however it was not that easy as marketing and selling a book that nobody was aware of through offline sellers was a tedious and time-consuming job.

Time passed by and then something came into existence that changed the whole cycle of selling and buying process. Online marketing and selling was the technique that got adopted by a lot of authors and publishers wherein they found selling their electronic Books online on different platforms and getting paid for the same, directly through online transactions

There is a lot to know about "how to sell an eBook on different platforms" however we would be talking about the most popular platform right now and that is Amazon. There is a series of steps that need to be taken to get the desired output and they are as follows:

Create an Amazon KDP Account:
The starter here is creating a Kindle Direct Publishing account on Amazon. The link that can be used to sign up:
https://kdp.amazon.com/self-publishing/signin
No worries if an EBook is not in Mobi/Kindle format as after uploading the book it would eventually get converted into the compatible Kindle format.

Add Books to the Bookshelf:
The next step that needs to be performed is adding an EBook to the bookshelf. On the Left-hand side of the dashboard after you are signed

There is a lot to know about "how to sell an eBook on different platforms" however we would be talking about the most popular platform right now and that is Amazon.

in, you will see an option of "Add New Title". Clicking on this option will take you to the page where you need to add the Book details.

The fields are quite self-explanatory however there are options to help you filling each field in case needed Enter your Book details and leave the ISBN (International Standard Book Number) field blank in case you do not have that info. Mention your name as well in case you are self-publishing the EBook.

Next, you need to choose the category you feel your book should reside in and the keywords as well that may help the readers find the desired content.

After all the above mentioned steps are done, you need to upload the cover image for your EBook which is as important as the EBook itself because this is the image that will be shown on Amazon Sale Page and would be a reflection of your content.

Uploading the EBook on the platform:
You can either upload a Kindle formatted eBook or a PDF/word format and let Amazon do the conversion for your EBook. If you are letting Amazon do the conversion thing then make sure you recheck the file for the pictures or graphics as converting online may disturb the formatting.

Confirm Your Pricing & Royalty Options:
You need to decide on the royalty option that you want to go for because the rest will be taken by Amazon.
There are 2 royalty options that you can select from:
35%
70%
If you want to keep 70% then you need to sell your book between $2.99 and $9.99. If the price is out of this range then you will only be getting 35% of the total selling price so beware and make sure you target the right pricing so that the return to your pocket is more.

You are done. Be a spectator, wait and watch. Let Amazon review your content and approve it. Once it's approved, the EBook will be published and the direct link will be shared with you.

Source: http://www.globalebookconversion.com/
EzineArticles.com

NEW YORKERS:
A FEISTY PEOPLE WHO WILL UNSETTLE, MADDEN, AMUSE AND ASTONISH YOU

Providing a narrative which flows well, as Author Clifford Browder employs a friendly, authentically knowledgeable tone, within which he gives literate life to a multilayered perspective of New York, through his work in this book.

By Lisa Brown Gilbert

When it comes to New York City, its dynamic environ and multicultural fusion of distinctive inhabitants, author Clifford Browder focuses his keen literary eye on his life and experiences as a seasoned resident there, as well as providing glimpses of the eclectic history of the city in his recent work, New Yorkers: A Feisty People Who will Unsettle, Madden, Amuse and Astonish You. Moreover, being no stranger to using the backdrop of New York as a setting for his previously published books, including a series set in nineteenth-century New York, titled Metropolis, author Browder once again provides an intriguing exploration of a very culturally distinctive locale.

Moreover, this is not your typical cut and dry biography, providing dry facts; instead, the read is a heartfelt memoir of a man and the city he lives, loves, survives and works in. The narrative keeps you rapt in its pages with a winning combination of information gleaned from Mr. Browder's unique standpoint, research, and experiences from his many years as a resident. Consequently, author Browder does well with transfixing the mental eye with descriptions of his life as a longtime resident, including historical glimpses and insider tidbits of the better-known aspects of New York as well as the lesser-known and even the obscure.

Providing a narrative which flows well, as Author Clifford Browder employs a friendly, authentically knowledgeable tone, within which he gives literate life to a multilayered perspective of New York, through his work in this book. In no particular chronological order, the text is divided into five parts with each section bringing into focus an intriguing variety of elements.

Firstly, Part one includes topics covering looks into the many people, languages, the hustlers, scavengers and the rich. Next, Part 2 looks at how New Yorkers live with chapters including; Fun, Booze, Smells, and Graffiti just to name a few. However, also included within this section is my favorite chapter #16, Are New Yorkers Rude? I think author Browder explored this question in fine style. Consecutively, Part 4 covers some of the more iconic locales including Broadway, Fifth Avenue, The Bowery, Wall street and 14th street. Part four continues with a tour of some of the museums, statues as well as an obscure but interest-piquing, whiskey-tasting cemetery. Followed by Part 5 which delves into some of the past history of New York, providing the insightful histories of both the good and the bad.

Overall, I enjoyed reading New Yorkers. Author Clifford Browder gave a fascinating insiders tour of New York. Part biography, part historical dive and part travel guide, this work offers a tantalizing vision of an exciting city overflowing with diversity in all respects. This was a worthwhile read which I do recommend. However, as a fellow New Yorker, I experienced some turbulent emotions while reading this book particularly with the advent of Coronavirus and the current lockdown in NY and all those wonderful people locked inside of their homes because of a virus. My heart and prayers go out to my family and friends as well as the author, his family and all other New Yorkers-God Bless Us All.

Source: EzineArticles

A Feisty People Who Will Unsettle,
Madden, Amuse and Astonish You

New Yorkers

Clifford Browder

Book Review of Robin Lamont's The Experiment

By Lisa Brown Gilbert

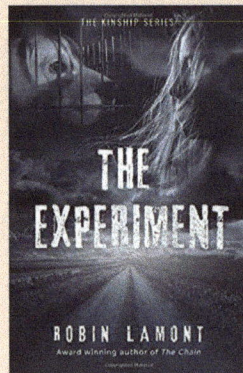

Robin Lamont's The Experiment, the third addition to her well-received Kinship series, traverses the rough terrain of animal rights in a story that not only takes readers seamlessly into a world that brims with webbed mystery but also exposes the horrific aspects of a subject that is not often visited - the protection of animals.

Promptly, from the narrative's outset, the suspense begins to build, as we meet the story's engagingly complex protagonist, Jude Brannock, a senior investigator at The Kinship, an organization specializing in undercover investigations of large scale / industrial animal abuse. Jude anxiously broods about a recently hired investigator, Time Mains her trainee, who suddenly seemed to be mysteriously missing in action. Investigative Trainee Tim Mains embarked on an independent mission to go undercover to gather, document and report violations at a targeted company Amaethon Industries. After a spate of little to no contact from Tim, Jude embarks on an intense mission to find the missing investigator determined to get to the truth of his whereabouts, especially after his cryptic message of being on to "something big". However, Jude's interest in the mystery of Tim's disappearance turns out to be more than just a "platonic" or "comrade in arms" type of concern for him as it turns out the two had started an affair that had to be kept out of sight.

Meanwhile, as the progress of her investigative efforts continues, Jude finds herself confronting a debilitating personal health issue. Her intimate feelings towards Tim brought on a deepening mystery as she hears evidence of his untoward behavior, including drug use, and an intense romance with a young woman, all while he was supposed to be working undercover investigating. It was now clear to her that Tim may not have been the man she thought she could trust not only with an important heartfelt job and not to mention with her heart.

Fundamentally, as a whole, The Experiment turned out to be a good stand-alone read that I found to be both creative and satisfying as a mystery read. Ultimately, the story captivated me with a mystery that deepened and twisted as the plot progressed centered around subject matter that I personally found a refreshing relief from the usual mystery genre fare. And as for characterizations, I found Jude to be a well-crafted central character whose own complex personal history intrigued, just as much as the other mysterious elements within the narrative which author Robin Lamont did a splendid job of culminating, into a cohesive and intriguing work that wielded suspense well. I look forward to her other books as well as hoping to see The Experiment made into a movie. I think it would be great and this book is definitely a must-read.

Book Review of The Dumb Class by Mike Hatch

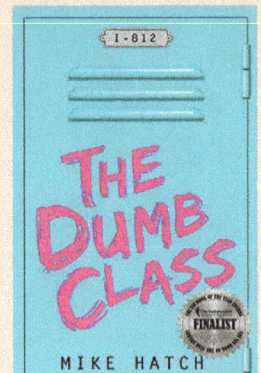

Author Mike Hatch delivers originality and spunk with his The Dumb Class: Boomer Junior High; a retrospective coming of age story that unflinchingly provides readers with a gritty, humorous, and boldly creative romp through life with a group of Junior High school friends.

Taking place in the 1960s, the story follows "baby Boomer" friends Bill Jones, Eddie, Jeff, and Harley through their formative years in Boomer Junior High school. Events are detailed by Bill Jones who is also the story's protagonist. As a whole, the teens are a cast of tenacious, drinking, smoking, sexing and scheming set of youth whose friendships and wit carry them through many escapades and life experiences. Jones, in particular, makes for a captivating character to follow. He has wit and a peculiar charm and albeit. Although in the lowest of the class designations in the junior high school, "the dumb class" he seems to be one of the smartest and conniving. Instantly intriguing from its outset the story draws your attention along with piquing the interest with an opening scene of a crudely humorous debate about the female anatomy, being held by the group of friends, which serves to bring the diverse main players into focus and sets the tone for the story as one replete with humor, raw depictions of life and teen behavior. As the story progresses, it follows their adventures, experiences, and explorations fueled by raunchy desires, cursing, teen angst, drugs, alcohol as well as other diversions like revenge. As characters, their unique personalities and interactions drive the story forward, while heralding authenticity via infused bits of historical and cultural references.

Overall, I found that The Dumb Class: Boomer Junior High offers not only an entertaining read but a multifaceted look at the cultural and sociological avenues of life that teenagers of the 1960's encountered and explored. As a matter of fact, I personally found the story to be a somewhat reminiscent combination of Stand By Me, Grease and Porkies. Just a word of warning, this is an adult-themed read as the level of sexuality in this book is quite graphic especially for fourteen and fifteen-year-olds. However overall, I enjoyed the read and kudos to author Mike Hatch, who did well in portraying his tale. He artfully brought this memorable coming of age story to life with humor, well-fleshed characters and era-appropriate vernacular. I do recommend this book for mature readers who enjoy dark themed humor.

1001 Movies You Must See Before You Die by Steven Jay Schneider

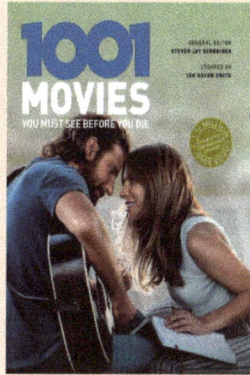

By Santhanam Nagarajan

The book under review 1001 Movies You Must See Before You Die edited by Steven Jay Schneider gives you details of 1001 famous movies released between 1900 and 2016.

It is an elaborate work and a film lover's dream.

It chronicles the entire history of cinema spread over hundred years. Choosing 1001 films from thousands of films is itself a research work and this was done by the author in a fantastic way.

How these films are chosen? First, from various best films, top hundred films, top ten movies lists 1300 films were selected. After going through the list again and again it was cut short to 1001 movies. The films list is given alphabetically at the beginning of the book.

For example if you choose Tom Tykwer's Run Lola Run, a 1998 film, you will get all the details.

Run Lola Run is an interesting, unusual film making experiment that has humor, breathless excitement and tremendous energy all tightly packaged into an MTV generation movie by the fresh talent of its writer-director.

The film shows the twenty minute story of Lola in three different times each subtly different in a manner that delivers three different outcomes. A beautiful innovative film's full details are given in a fitting manner.

Like this you may read about one thousand and one best films and start viewing one by one before your death.

The Genre index given at the end of the book covers 22 subjects namely Action, Adventure, Animation, Avant-Garde, Comedy, Crime, Docu-drama, Documentary, Drama, Experimental, Family, Fantasy, Horror, Musical, Mystery, Noir, Romance, Sci-fi, Short, Thriller, War and Western.

The directors index gives you details about 596 famous director including Cecil B. Demille, Alfred Hitchcock, Steven Spielberg etc.

War films such The Bridge on the river Kwai (1957), The Great Escape (1963), Gone with the Wind (1939) needs to be specially mentioned here.

However we are not able to find the famous war films such The Guns of Navarone, Force Ten from Navarone etc.

Movies like The Italian Job are also not covered in this list.

Perhaps if we have to include all the films the title will become 10001 Movies you must see before you die!

Scientific Fiction films are also narrated elaborately.

The book is printed very neatly in art paper. Hundreds of illustration makes the reader very happy.

We may see and choose our favorite stars, Directors and we could make our own list based on our interest.

More than hundred years, the film field in one of the most entertaining one and we can't imagine a world without movies now.

So we have to congratulate the General Editor Steven Jay Schneider for his painstaking work. He is a film critic, Scholar, and producer. He has written many books on the Cinematic arts.

Damn Good Advice

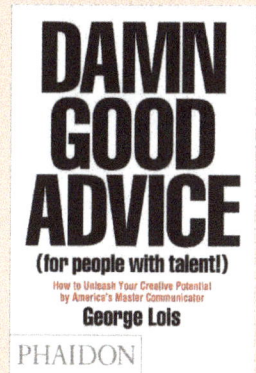

The book under review titled 'Damn Good Advice' written by the Ad Guru George Lois has been written based on his experience and hence worth reading.

It is a well-known fact that Lois is a Supernova, the original Mr Big Idea. Since 1950's he has had a titanic influence on world culture.

He has 120 valuable tips to lead a creative and successful life.

Lois was born in New York in 1931.He is an advertising legend and the creator of Big Idea advertising.

Lois first wants the leader to identify himself choosing the type to which he belongs to.

There are only four types of persons.

1) Very bright, Industrious (You are perfect)
2) Very bright, lazy (A damn shame)
3) Stupid, lazy (You are a wash)
4) Stupid, industrious (You are dangerous)

He cautions us, 'If you are number 1 or a 2, you will get a lot out of this book. If your are a number 3 or 4, you need not read this book.' Very true.

All the tools in the world are meaningless without an essential idea. Hence always go for a big idea. Whatever you want to communicate to the world it should be communicated in a nanosecond. He quotes Lincoln who did not have time to contemplate, correct and edit his letter wrote a very long letter to his friend and express his apology citing the above reasons!

Energy begets energy. Playing War games may help you. Sports and the intense intellectualism of the game of chess help drive and sustain the creative ethos. Lois quotes Thomas Huxley. "The chessboard is the world, the pieces are the phenomena of the universe, the rules of the game are what we call the laws of Nature."

Age is not a barrier. Charles Darwin was 50 when he wrote On The Origin of Species.

At 52, Ray Kroc started MacDonald.

A.C.Bhakthivedanta Swami Prabhupada founded the Hare Krishna movement when he was 69, with $7 to his name.

A little courage is needed. A great deal of talent is lost to the world for want of a little courage. The Webster dictionary zeroes in on the meaning of the word "courage", marked by bold resolution in withstanding the dangerous, alarming or difficult.. a firmness of spirit that faces danger or extreme difficulty without flinching or retreating. And in his 120th advice he recalls the sufferings of Nelson Mandela. While incarcerated at Robben Island and Pollsmoor prisons for 27 years, recited Invictus, the iconic poem written in 1875 by the English poet William Ernest Henley to his fellow prisoners, empowering all with its message of self mastery. The last four lines of the poem is worth remembering ever:

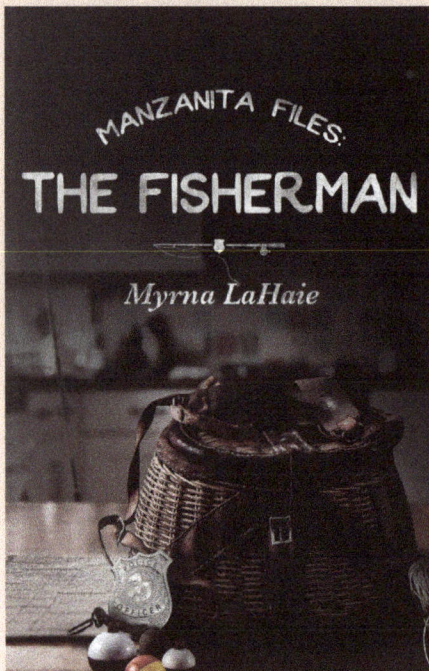

Recent release "Manzanita Files: The Fisherman" from Newman Springs Publishing author Myrna LaHaie is the thrilling tale of Sherry Ortiz, who receives a job offer from a former boss, pleading for her help in the drug-filled town he is now presiding over.

Author Myrna LaHaie's New Book 'Manzanita Files: The Fisherman' is the Mysterious Story of a Decorated Police Sergeant Who Takes on a New Job as a Fresh Start for Herself and Her Son

in a wonderful climate, with shivers running down her spine as she found out within only a couple of days that it looked like she had made a huge mistake. The murder of a police sergeant, a disappearing chief, some suspicious officers, an intermittent supply of drugs, and death make her world appear to crumble as it endangers those she serves and cares for. Readers who wish to experience this gripping work can purchase "Manzanita Files: The Fisherman" at bookstores everywhere, or online at the Apple iBooks Store, Amazon, or Barnes and Noble.

For additional information or media inquiries, contact Newman Springs Publishing at 732-243-8512.

About Newman Springs Publishing:

Newman Springs Publishing is a full-service publishing house for serious authors. Each title produced by Newman Springs Publishing undergoes every step of the professional publishing process, including editing, layout, cover design, circulation, distribution, and publicity. All titles are made available in both eBook and print formats. Newman Springs Publishing distributes to tens of thousands of retail outlets throughout North America and internationally. All manuscripts in any genre are welcome to be submitted for review; If the manuscript meets the necessary criteria and is accepted for publication, Newman Springs Publishing will work closely with the author to bring the book to the retail market for a relatively inexpensive initial investment.

SAMUEL LUGEIYAMU MUTASA
DipEd, Cert. R. S., BSc., MSc.

CHILD UPBRINGING
The Pivotal Role of Mothers in Various Cultures and Religions

Recent release "Child Upbringing" from Covenant Books author Samuel Lugeiyamu Mutasa is an insightful account that delves into the efficacy of nurturing the youth and responsible parenthood for a better society.

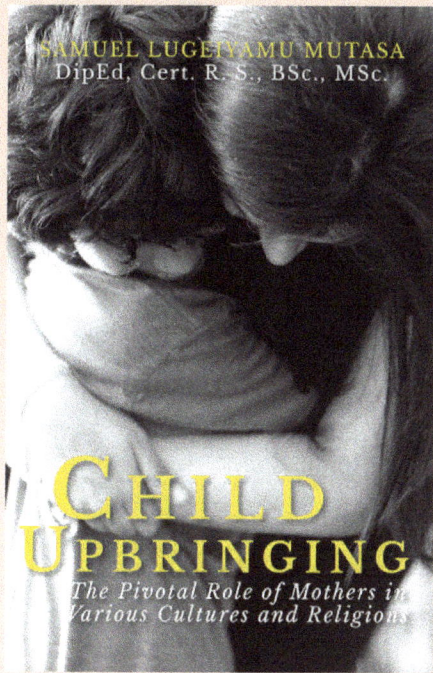

Samuel Lugeiyamu Mutasa's New Book 'Child Upbringing' is an Intellectual Read on Proper Child Upbringing and Parental Guidance

and left them near death.

This story depicts how they survived through the excellent care of the trauma team at Osceola Hospital and through their arduous journey of coming back. It also describes how their children traveled more than eight hundred miles to step in to deal with hospital personnel and make important decisions regarding their care and survival. While hospital staff could not believe, the first one to reach their bedside was their pastor Dan Hopkins from Virginia. Dottie and Skip were not at all surprised. They believe God orchestrated their survival and recovery through excellent hospital personnel, family and friends. They also believe that God spared the young mother and her three young children from any injuries that day."

Published by Christian Faith Publishing, Dorothy Megee's new book is an inspiring read that shows a heartwarming healing journey and the hope and love that brings people together.

View a synopsis of "A Beautiful Day, a Crash, and a Thousand Blessings" on YouTube.

Consumers can purchase "A Beautiful Day, a Crash, and a Thousand Blessings" at traditional brick & mortar bookstores, or online at Amazon.com, Apple iTunes store, or Barnes and Noble.

The Body
A GUIDE FOR OCCUPANTS
By BILL BRYSON

Category: Science | Humor
Oct 15, 2019 |
ISBN 9780385539302

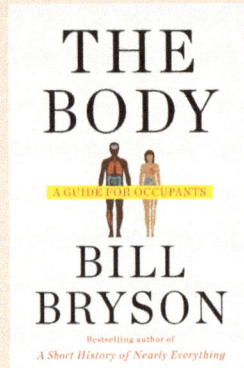

"A directory of wonders. . .Extraordinary. . . A tour of the minuscule; it aims to do for the human body what his A Short History of Nearly Everything did for science. . .The prose motors gleefully along, a finely tuned engine running on jokes, factoids and biographical interludes. . .Wry, companionable, avuncular and always lucid . . .[The Body] could stand as an ultimate prescription for life."
—The Guardian

"Bill Bryson isn't a medic, biologist or psychiatrist, but that's what makes his exploration of the human body, all seven billion billion billion atoms of it (the book is rich in jaw-dropping stats), so readable and useful. As with his earlier A Short History of Nearly Everything, which offers a non-specialist introduction to science, he asks all the questions a layperson doesn't dare to ask for fear of exposing humiliating ignorance, then answers them in witty, jargon-free prose that glides you through 400 pages. . .It's fun to read because it's not just comprehensive, but quirky. . .Bryson thrives."
—The Times (London)

"Bill Bryson is not so much a discoverer of new lands as a charismatic cartographer of existing ones, smartly mapping points of entry into territory that might otherwise remain impenetrable to curious travelers. With light footed prose, The Body winds its way through the dense terrain of anatomy, physiology, and biochemistry. . .The result is an absorbing catalog of the human body in all its firmness and fatality. . .The colossal roster of facts on display is dazzling. . . Bryson's distinctive voice will likely delight readers eager to go sightseeing around the world they embody."
—The American Scholar

The Book of Dust: The Secret Commonwealth (Book of Dust, Volume 2)
By PHILIP PULLMAN

Category: Teen & Young Adult Fantasy Fiction | Teen & Young Adult Fiction | Teen & Young Adult Action & Adventure

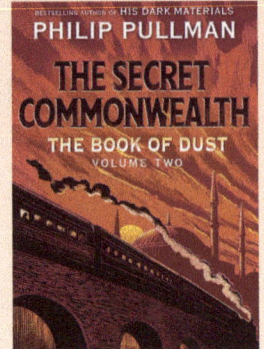

Oct 03, 2019 | ISBN 9780553510669 | Young Adult

"The Secret Commonwealth is a majestic return to Lyra's next chapter with all the magic, folklore, and fantasy only Philip Pullman can provide." –Hypable

"A big novel full of big ideas, big characters and big sorrows. . . This book feels like a response to the darkness of our time."—NPR

"The novel gallops forward, full of danger, delight and surprise. Pullman is a staggeringly gifted storyteller."
—New Statesman

"Not only is it worthy second instalment in The Book of Dust trilogy, it continues to prove this sequence will be every bit as excellent as His Dark Materials."—Seattle Post-Intelligencer

"Mr. Pullman's writing is clear, clean and forceful, never striving for effect and all the more effective because of it. He's also a man of ideas, which gives great savor to his work." – The Wall Street Journal

"Engrossing."—Financial Timesst, the Pulitzer Prize and a TV miniseries starring Frances McDormand, Olive Kitteridge is surely the most beloved unlikable character in recent literary history. . . . This new collection of stories about Olive's friends and family hits it out of the park."—Newsday

Bloody Genius
By JOHN SANDFORD

Category: Crime Mysteries | Suspense & Thriller

Oct 01, 2019 | ISBN 9780525536611

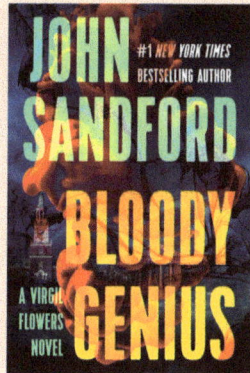

"[A] smartly plotted mystery."—New York Times Book Review

More Praise for Bloody Genius

"Sandford is a terrific storyteller who can spin an intriguing tale without having to fill it with death-defying mayhem. . .Armchair sleuths who are intent on solving the crime for themselves will need to be on their toes."—Minneapolis Star Tribune

"Compulsively readable. . . Readers who like a bit of unrepentant wiseass in their sleuths will find Flowers fits the bill. Sandford makes blending humor and mystery look easy."—Publishers Weekly

"Flowers remains one of the great modern fictional detectives, and Sandford, as always, supplies amazing secondary characters, sharp dialogue, and plots that confound and amaze. A near-perfect crime novel."—Booklist (starred review)

"[A] fast-paced, intensifying adventure. As always, the investigation is intricately plotted, while details of Flowers's family life are included for fans of the character. . .
The irreverent humor and language is perfect for the unconventional law officer in the darkly entertaining series."—Library Journal (starred review)

"[Sandford] appears to have no shortage of story ideas. More impressively, he continues to execute them brilliantly. . .Another dazzling whodunit."—The Real Book Spy

"Steadily absorbing revelations of all manner of malfeasance, beautifully handled."—Kirkus Reviews

Fair Play
A GAME-CHANGING SOLUTION FOR WHEN YOU HAVE TOO MUCH TO DO (AND MORE LIFE TO LIVE)
By EVE RODSKY

Category: Personal Growth

Oct 01, 2019 | ISBN 9780525541936

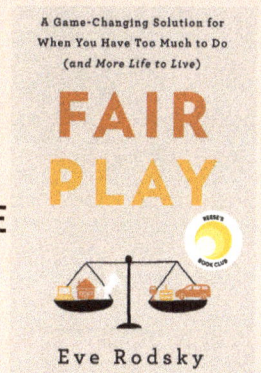

"A hands-on strategy to divide tasks and achieve household harmony."—Real Simple

"[An] impressive debut…Couples searching for ways to better manage their families and achieve a balance of domestic work will benefit from Rodsky's actionable strategy."—Publishers Weekly

"Rodsky's system, which uses task cards divided between partners, is potentially revolutionary and [Fair Play] offers the right combination of venting and commiserating balanced by practical solutions and manageable approaches to tough conversations…poised to become a book-club favorite."—Booklist

"Watch out for Eve Rodsky. Reese Witherspoon's media company, Hello Sunshine, has annointed her as the Marie Kondo of relationships, and we think they might be on to something."—BookPage

"A must read for every busy woman out there."—PopSugar's Best Books of Fall

"I'm so impressed with the Fair Play handbook. Not only did Eve break down every task that a couple is responsible for, but she managed to create a system where dividing those tasks is fun, insightful and gratifying. Her approach is filled with love, humor, wisdom and the idea that if we can work together and acknowledge each other's strengths and weaknesses, we can build better, stronger, and longer lasting relationships."—Reese Witherspoon

The Things We Don't Talk About:

A Memoir of Hardships, Healing, and Hope

New Book Sheds Heartfelt Light on Many Taboo Topics

Ogden, UT, USA— In her highly anticipated debut novel, nationally-acclaimed speaker and disruptor Stacy Bernal tackles some weighty topics, such as childhood sexual abuse, suicide, autism parenting, and breast implant illness in a surprisingly heartfelt and humorous way in The Things We Don't Talk About: A Memoir of Hardships, Healing, and Hope.

"As I've traveled around the country speaking at events, I've discovered that no matter where I go there are always so many people who share parallel journeys and similar stories to my own," Bernal said. "I've met some incredible people who have inspired me to write this book and share my story, in the hopes that it will create ripple effects of positive change for other people who may be struggling with similar issues as me."

Bernal began her speaking career in March of 2017, when she shared her story of 'Failure to Finisher' about how running her first marathon in 2009 changed her life. At the time, she was a three-time divorced, three-time college dropout on government assistance and was barely able to afford rent and groceries for herself

and her autistic son.

At her very lowest point, she found herself feeling utterly hopeless about life. She credits running her first 26.2-mile race as a literal lifesaver. From there, she redirected the course of her life, going back to college in 2010 where she eventually graduated Summa Cum Laude at 36-years-old.

Her memoir chronicles the lessons she learned throughout her years of hardships: how shame and trauma from childhood abuse silenced her and created insurmountable limiting self-beliefs, and how overcoming the odds transformed her mindset. Through authentic storytelling and wholehearted living, she found peace and empowerment. Those lessons have helped Bernal help others. "I feel like every horrible, painful experience from my past has served a purpose in helping me become who I am today," said Bernal. In 2018, she started an autism awareness event in her community and in 2019 she founded a 501(c)(3) nonprofit, Bernal Badassery Foundation. "I really want to pay it forward and help others who are struggling," she said.

Announcing the debut book for speaker, nonprofit founder, and disruptor Stacy Bernal.

Stacy Bernal has been featured on Thrive Global, HER Magazine, Autism Parenting Magazine, and Scary Mommy. She has spoken around the country for school districts, women's groups, and corporate trainings. She is a founding member for the US chapter of the global organization, KeyNote Women Speakers. When she isn't speaking or writing, she's playing with kids and fur babies, going for a run, or tackling the never-ending pile of laundry.

The Mother of Coaching
CHÉRIE CARTER-SCOTT

The Mother of Coaching Since 1974. Trains & Licenses Professional Coaches World-wide. Oprah Endorsed. New York Times Best Selling Author, Fortune 500 Business Coach Consultant. Expert in Customer Service & Overcoming Negativity.

BY ANNA HARLOWE
March 8, 2021
BANGKOK- THAILAND

Tell us a bit about the beginnings of the coaching industry?

In 1974 I was searching my mind, heart, and soul for the purpose of my life, when a colleague asked me if I could help him sort out some issues regarding his company. I had little to no experience with business and couldn't imagine what value I could bring to his situation. I declined his invitation and continued my quest for meaning and relevance. He called two additional times and asked if I could help him. I was becoming mildly irritated and asked him, "Why are you calling me?" To wit he replied, "Because I trust you." I protested, "But I don't know anything." He retorted, "That could come in handy!" I was dismayed and stated, "If you completely understand that I know nothing about your business, and you are willing to pay me to help you sort out some issues, then I accept!"

In October, 1974, we started the project and Lloyd became my first official coaching client. After a successful coaching assignment, he started sharing his amazing results with everyone he came in contact with…it sounded like, "My friend, Cherie, the woman who asks the incredibly powerful questions." My phone started to ring off the hook. Before I knew it, I was coaching people every day, more and more called, and even though I continued to protest, "I don't know anything about business, but I will ask you questions and you will discover your own answers." They didn't care that I claimed to know nothing, because the recommendation from Lloyd (and others) was so emphatic.

In 1974, I charged $35 for a 90-minute session. Within six months, clients started to ask if I could teach them how to ask those powerful questions in order to work more effectively with their patients, customers, and clients. The answer to their request was unclear to me since I was unaware of what I was doing in those sessions that was so profoundly helpful to people. I knew I helped them focus, determine what they wanted, and make clear choices, however, I had no idea how the combination of intention, skills, abilities, and the use of positive energy created such extraordinary results. People used the word, "Gifted" to describe what I did, however, like a prodigy, the "not-knowing mindset" came naturally to me, without effort or performance anxiety.

With the help of my friend, Kathy, we started to examine and analyze what I was doing that was creating the amazing results. The most important aspect was that I was absolutely certain that I didn't

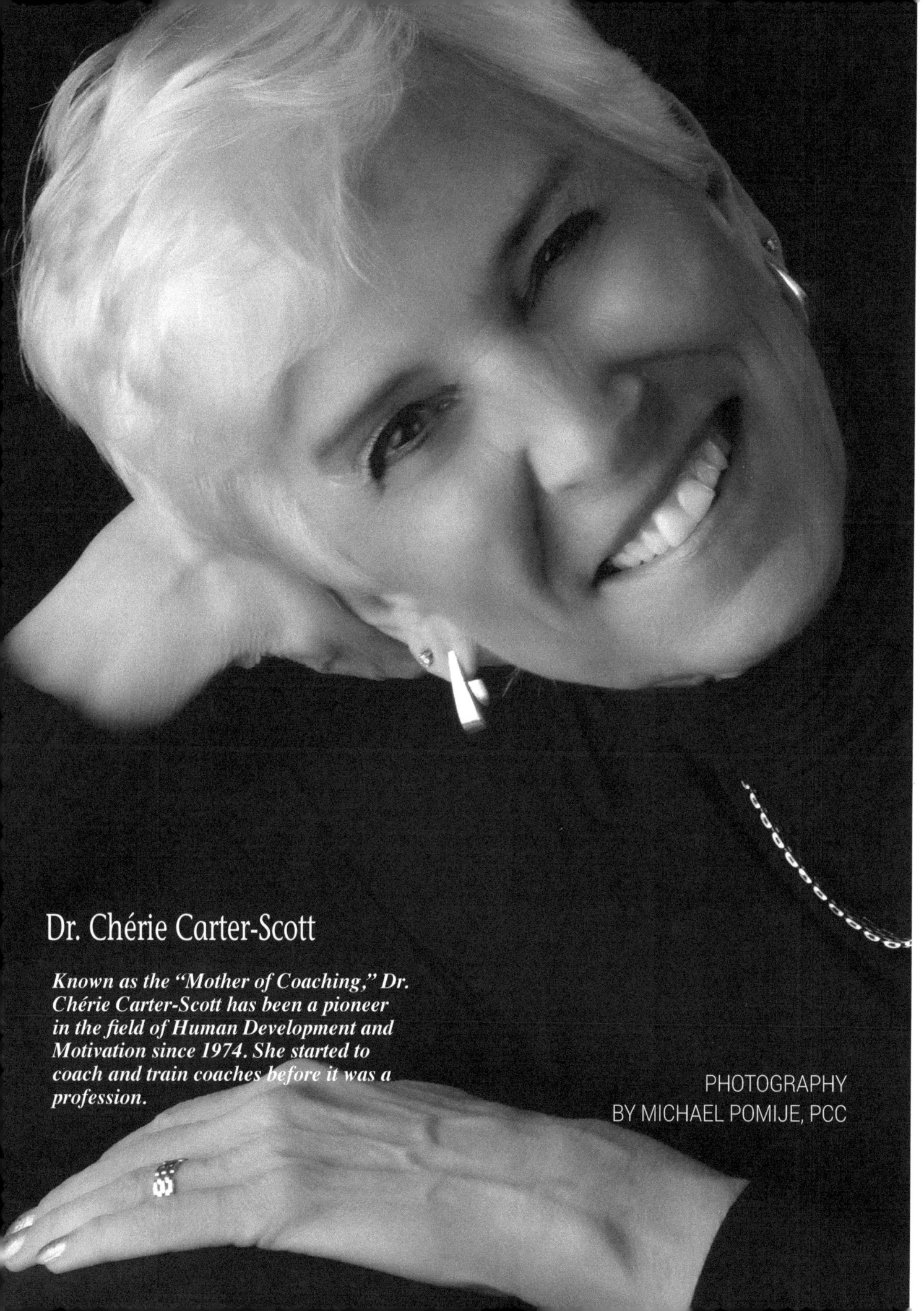

Dr. Chérie Carter-Scott

Known as the "Mother of Coaching," Dr. Chérie Carter-Scott has been a pioneer in the field of Human Development and Motivation since 1974. She started to coach and train coaches before it was a profession.

own answers to all of their challenges, and I never presumed to know for anyone else what their choices or actions should be. This was the perfect starting place, and from there Kathy assessed everything I did with my clients that had worked. The initial behaviors were obvious and she immediately noticed that I easily suspended judgment, something Kathy said was not so easy to do. I didn't know that setting aside judgments was challenging for others, and so we set out to find the root of judgmental behavior in order to unlock that mechanism. If I could suspend judgment, I imagined that it must be possible for others to do so, as well, however, we needed to determine how to unlock the judgmental mechanism? In addition to suspending judgment, we had to find a way to train people to not know the answer for others. Since this was a knee-jerk reaction, trained over many years of formal educational environments, we believed that it would take a concerted effort to reverse this deeply-ingrained behavior.

We thought that if an individual exhumed their own dreams, they might experience the process from the inside out and be more attuned to the fragility of the human psyche and emotions. In other words, if they experienced the process of remembering their precious dreams, they might be more respectful of the dreams, wishes, and goals of others.

Listening Actively was essential to the process, but how could you listen if your mind was busy chattering at you?

We needed to find ways to help people silence the voices of their mind, at least temporarily, for an hour or so, so that the coach could listen intensely and focus on what was being said. This focus of attention was critically important. We queried, 'How could we get their attention off of themselves and 100% on to another person?' (A critical concern)

Then there were those powerful questions that I asked that seemed to come out of thin air. When Kathy asked me how I found those questions, I commented that as I listened intently to their answers, the next question magically presented itself. If I was paying close attention to what was stated, the "Clue" would surface and reveal itself to me. If my mind were elsewhere, I would surely miss it. As we proceeded with the analysis of my behaviors that created a safe coaching environment, more elements started to surface. Kathy noticed that I used the techniques of restating and recapping frequently. I was unaware of this, but acknowledged that I wanted

to ensure that I really understood what was had been communicated to me, and to confirm that we were both on the same page as we progressed together. Although I didn't want to be irritating to the client, I really wanted to make sure that I hadn't missed something or lost the thread. Kathy commented that I never gave advice, and I shared with her that since I knew nothing about the client's situation, it would have been presumptuous or arrogant of me to imagine that I had any advice that might be remotely helpful. I commented, "Listening closely in a non-judgmental manner, reflecting back what I heard, asking questions that go deeper, and being very respectful of the client's inner wishes, dreams, and fears just about summed it up." Kathy was also respectful when she requested to sit in on a session with a client and watch what I did to determine if there was more that I was unaware of. I obtained permission from a client and Kathy watched silently in the corner, with her clipboard in hand. After the session, she commented, "I have a whole new list of behaviors that I observed." She continued to list the behaviors, of me, the "Unconscious Competent," a person who is unaware of their extraordinary capabilities. Kathy commented, "You were sincerely interested and

curious about your client's situation, and you asked several times about their feelings regarding related items. You were very connected to the client and if the connection became shaky, you took it on yourself to repair any disconnection. There was an interesting blend of caring coupled with empowerment. You weren't weak or mushy, nor were you pushy or forceful. You didn't get shaken when feelings came to the surface, which was impressive, and although empathetic, you didn't take on their feelings or get enmeshed in them. How did you do that?" she questioned. I wasn't really sure how to answer that, I was aware of the boundaries: where I ended and where the client began, which helped to see clearly that their feelings were not mine. Kathy continued to list the many behaviors that I demonstrated, and eventually we had a rather lengthy list. This was the first step in the process. Then I enlisted the help of a new colleague, Carol, who

helped me design the first MMS Coach Training in the Fall of 1974. Carol was the ideal associate because she was curious, enthusiastic, collaborative, and non-judgmental. We took the list from Kathy and set out on the mission…to design a training to teach people how to coach their clients, patients, and customers in the same way I was coaching them.

What is life coaching?

As the International Coaching Federation defines it: "Coaching is partnering with clients in a thought-provoking and creative process that inspires them to maximize their personal and professional potential.' This is the broadest and most inclusive definition.

What's involved in coaching?
Establishing the coaching agreement is critical so both people: coach and client are on the same page, have clear expectations about the nature of the conversation(s), what will and won't be addressed, and what the approach would be. It was also important in managing expectations to address what is not coaching, specifically: mentoring, advising, consulting, and therapy.

How does it work?

> "We thought that if an individual exhumed their own dreams, they might experience the process from the inside out and be more attuned to the fragility of the human psyche and emotions."

Coaching combines a variety of approaches starting with Socrates and his belief that questioning rather than telling leads to a more fruitful discovery of one's values and and priorities. Those who have contributed to the various components of coaching are:
• Socrates' open-ended questions
• Maria Montessori -Inner Knowing
• Carl Jung -Personality Theory
• Kurt Lewin -Freezing & Refreezing
• Joe Luft (1955) - Johari Window: Self-Awareness
• Harry Ingham (1955) - Johari Window: Self-Awareness
• Douglas McGregor -Theory X & Y
• Abraham Maslow: Hierarchy of Needs
• Carl Rogers -Active Listening
• Mihaly Csikszentmihalyi – Flow
• B.F. Skinner – Stimulus/Response Therapy
• Michael Neenan – adaptability
• Albert Ellis – changing belief systems
• David McClelland – 3 Motivators
• Daniel J. Levinson – People matter

- Frederick Hertzberg – Satisfaction and fulfillment
- Jack Mezirow – Unconscious Assumptions
- William Glasser – Choice Theory
- Louise Hay – Self-Love is the key
- Victor Vroom -Expectancy Theory
- Sir John Whitmore The GROW Model
- David Kolb Experiential Learning
- Martin Seligman – Positive Psychology
- Richard Barrett -Seven Levels
- Dr. Chérie Carter-Scott, MCC: Expectation Mgnt, DWBC (in document)
- Salovey and Mayer – EI & Monitoring Feelings

What are some of the most meaningful goals that your coaching has allowed clients to realize?

Changing jobs or careers, moving to a new location, finding one's soul-mate, increasing one's income or net worth, and a variety of smaller items like: time management, stress management, Finding the purpose of their lives is profound and includes context, direction, and fulfillment. Essentially, it connects the dots that the client has become aware of in their defining moments. Here is a short list of the types of goals that clients bring to coaching:
- Develop my self-confidence
- Speak up in meetings
- Learn to listen better
- Become more empathetic
- Get to bed earlier
- Be on time more often
- Manage stress effectively
- Stop procrastinating (a chronic case)
- Make more friends
- Become more disciplined (and structured)
- Keep my commitments (to myself and others)
- Stop being defensive (at performance reviews)
- Learn to network better at events (said by an introvert)
- Executive presence (gravitas)
- Transition from a manager to a leader
- Balancing work and home (said by a workaholic)
- Find a career/industry that I value and can make a difference in

What would you do to uncover subtle objectives that were not yet discernible to clients?

I would ask straight out do you hear this? Do you recognize this element? Does this resonate with you? I hear this, is that accurate in your perception?

Are there any objectives that are not amenable to life coaching?

Focus on the past traumas, phobias, strong addictions, any category that has been clinically labeled and studied as a condition that deviates from functional human being.

Which services would you recommend as adjuncts to coaching?

Personal development with all of the components, as long as they have the high value of the client, patient, customer having their own inner answers to their life's challenges.

Does a coach sort out the client's life?

No, the coach can ask the client to sort out their life, but the coach can offer to the client what they hear, see, observe, notice, perceive, or feel intuitively about the client of their circumstances.

What is the coach's role exactly?

A mirror, a sounding board, verbal reflection interaction, positive and constructive contextualizing, addressing any transition, decision-making and choice-making based on one's inner values and priorities.

Can anyone benefit from coaching?

IN theory, yes, but in actuality, they must have these four aspects:
Desire, Willingness, Belief, and Commitment. They also should be "above the line "in terms of Life Condition (DWBC)

And will I get results?

If the DWBC is solid there is a 98% chance of everything working perfectly with the client.

What's the difference between coaching, counselling, mentoring, and consulting?

- Coach: the person who is conducting the coaching session
- Client: the recipient (the team or group) in the coaching session
- Mentor: Advisor, guide, or subject matter expert
- Sponsor: the person who is financially responsible for the coaching engagement
- Sponsor Options: corporation, spouse, parent, mentor, or friend

How can coaching help me?

That depends on where you are in your life and where you want to go (grow). It depends on how ready, willing, and open you are to your coach, and the coaching process. It depends on your relationship with yourself, your honesty level, your pain points, and your urgency.

What sort of people have a life coach?

Those who see the value, the need, who want support in getting what they want, and those who can allocate the time, energy, and resources to this special connection and purpose.

What type people do you coach?

I coach the children of my clients, my students, my corporate clients, primarily those in the C-suite, those in my family, my licensees, leaders of my Coach Training, and people I am assigned through Mindspan, UNAIDS, and other agencies who broker coaches. (Please reference the Fixed vs. the Growth Mindset)

What made you choose life coach as a profession?

Actually, coaching chose me in 1974, as I have described in the beginning of this document.
 Tell us about your approach to life coaching and your specialty area?
- Executive coaching
- Transition coaching
- Life Purpose

Why are you so passionate about your work?

I am incredibly passionate about coaching because it is my life's purpose to support people being the very best version of themselves.
What does it cost?
It depends on whether it is personal or corporate, whether you are a student paying for yourself or the CEO of an MNC. The prices vary based on the coach's experience, years of coaching, credentials, and pricing packages.
Is coaching worth the price?
It depends on the results and the price of the coaching.

How do coaches help their clients get results?

Through sincere curiosity, the powerful questioning approach, summaries: restatement and recapping, empathetic unattached observations, the rock-solid belief in the client's abilities,

What kind of success have people you've coached gone on to have?

Transformation, clear and focused perspective. at all levels, fulfilling their life's purpose, fulfilling their destiny from an inner-directed place. ∎

Let's Go! is the children's version of amazon best-selling author, Larry Jacobson's adventure while navigating around the world in his yacht and is peppered with exciting fantasy and fiction. The story is filled with subtle lessons about anti-bullying, trust, friendship, giving, facing fears, and achieving one's dream in spite of obstacles. Parents, teachers, and librarians will appreciate the accurate geography as well as the auto-click Nautical Glossary in the Kindle Version.

et's Go! by Larry Jacobson offers excitement, adventure, and good solid life lessons for children ages 8-12.

Award-winning author, speaker, and adventurer, Larry Jacobson today released a new children's book, based on his six-time award-winning memoir, The Boy Behind the Gate, that recorded his six-year voyage of sailing around the world in his yacht, Julia. Let's Go! is the children's version of Jacobson's adventure and is peppered with light fantasy and fiction. The story is filled with subtle lessons about anti-bullying, trust, friendship, giving, facing fears, and achieving one's dream in spite of obstacles.

Parents, teachers, and librarians will appreciate the accurate geography as well as the auto-click Nautical Glossary in the Kindle Version. The story teaches good moral values, inspires confidence, and is fun and exciting for parents as well as children. The Kindle version, released at just $2.99 in the Amazon Kindle Store has 24 full color illustrations to supplement the imagination.

Jacobson said, "Mixing fiction with stories and memories from my adventure of sailing around the world was challenging at times, yet it was liberating to let my imagination go." At one point while struggling with a particular chapter, Jacobson's editor told him to 'Think like a 10-year old, that shouldn't be hard for you Larry!" And so the book was born.

Larry Jacobson

Larry Jacobson is an award-winning author, sought after motivational speaker, and leadership coach. He teaches the skills, traits and characteristics needed to achieve great accomplishments.

A California native, Jacobson grew up sailing and swimming on the beaches of the Pacific Ocean. A graduate of the University of California at Irvine, and Berkeley, he became a nationally recognized entrepreneur with 20 successful years in the business world. An avid sailor, he has over 50,000 blue water miles under his keel and authored the six-time award-winning memoir of his circumnavigation in the book, The Boy Behind the Gate. Jacobson's other books include ReDefine Your Retirement, and Navigating Entrepreneurship, 11 Proven Keys to Success.

He lives in the San Francisco Bay Area and welcomes new friends and inquiries at: www.larryjacobson.com

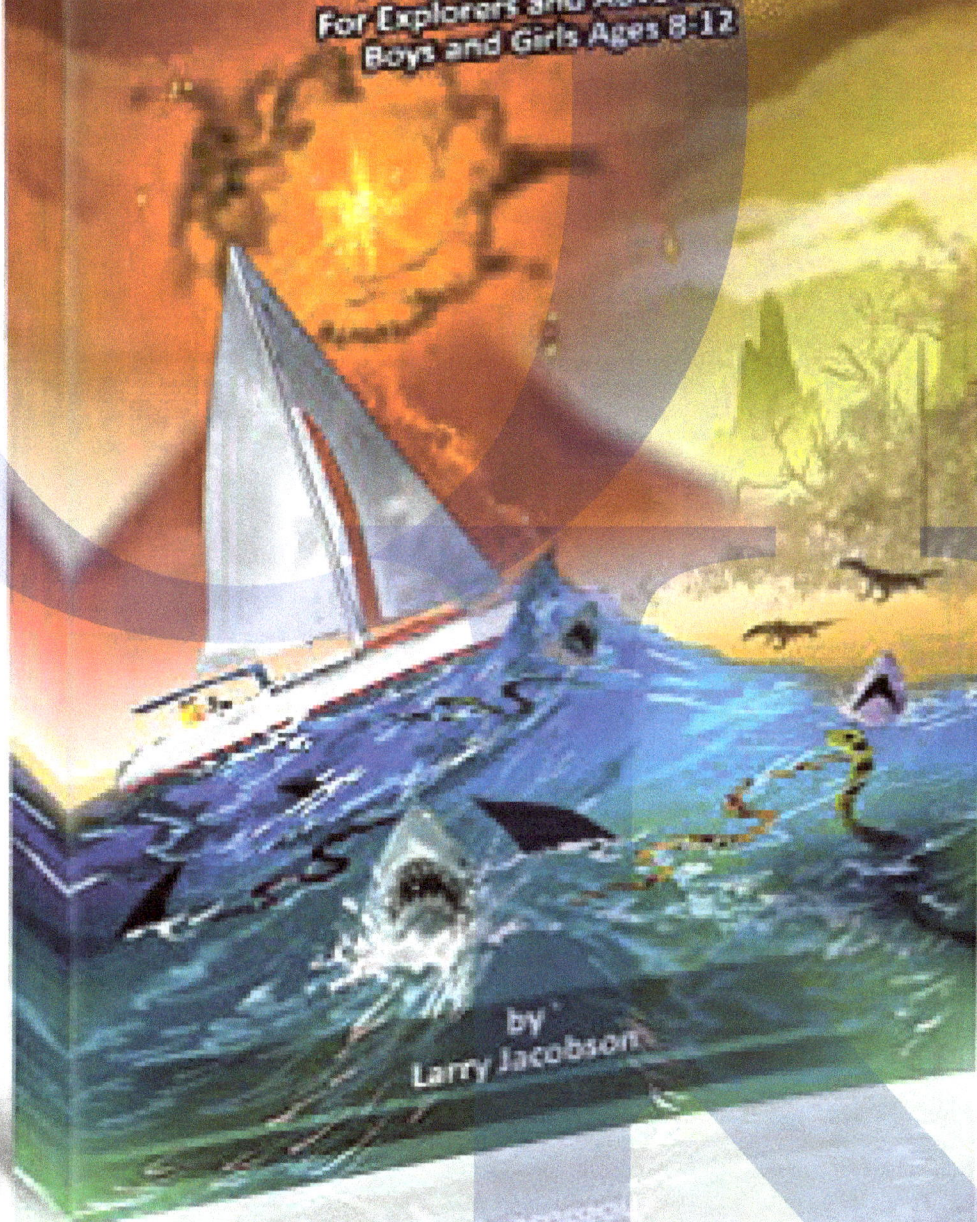

LET'S GO!

The Adventures of Skip and Kanek

Part I, The Search Begins
For Explorers and Adventurers
Boys and Girls Ages 8-12

by
Larry Jacobson

NEW YORK - Since every social media platform has a different culture, professionals need to understand the purpose and functions within each environment to best optimize the experience. As a follow up to his wildly successful "10 Powerful Networking Tips" series, Author and CEO Carl E. Reid launches a new book to leverage the power of social media in networking. Depending on each person's professional goals, every platform is not necessarily for everyone—meaning, a presence on all social media sites is not necessary to garner success. Reid's new book, 10 Powerful Networking Tips Using Social Media: Start Conversations And Attract Quality Lifetime Connections Power Networking In A Social Media World (ISBN 979-8623434067, paperback, 141 pp., 5.5 x 8.5 inches, 19.95), serves as a reference guide to help make connections using appropriate network etiquette.

"I started my management consulting company with a focus on technology and leadership development," shares Reid, CEO of Savvy Intrapreneur. "In addition to consulting services, we publish books for intrapreneurs, career professionals, and entrepreneurs to empower them to supercharge their survival success traveling through the uncertain business landscape of the 21st century."

Whether new to social media or experienced in power networking, 10 Powerful Networking Tips Using Social Media will help bring networking engagements to the next level and guide readers towards achieving their personal, career, or business goals. Ten social media platforms are covered

By Savvy Intrapreneur

10 POWERFUL NETWORKING TIPS
USING SOCIAL MEDIA

in great detail to provide a cross-section of different resources proven to work best for high-impact networking engagements. Following each chapter's title, the categories offered help readers to identify the platforms that may work best for their goals. Beyond the ten main networks covered, a comprehensive list of other global social media platforms is provided at the end of the book.

"This is a wonderful resource by Carl E. Reid," explains Christine Dykeman, Certified Human Resources Professional. "It's easy to read and understand, no matter what your prior experience is with social media. I highly recommend this book to everyone!"

The book is now available in a Kindle edition and paperback at 10SocialMediaNetworkingTips.com. For more information about 10 Powerful Networking Tips Using Social Media or the author Carl E. Reid, please visit CarlEReid.com or follow him on social media at Twitter.com/CarlEReid, LinkedIn.com/in/CarlEReid, Facebook.com/CarlEReid, and Instagram.com/CarlEReid.

SOURCE: PRLog -

CARL E. REID, CSI

10 POWERFUL NETWORKING TIPS USING SOCIAL MEDIA

START CONVERSATIONS AND ATTRACT QUALITY LIFETIME CONNECTIONS POWER NETWORKING IN A SOCIAL MEDIA WORLD

FOREWORD BY
BIBA PEDRON
THE CONNECTION QUEEN
[BEST SELLING AUTHOR]

PR Starter Kit

Whether you're a newbie or just need a refresher, it's always beneficial to review public relations basics

Whether you're a newbie to the world of public relations or just need a refresher, it's always beneficial to review public relations basics. As tools and technologies constantly evolve, the fundamentals of PR stay the same.

It's imperative that you bring agility, collaboration and planning to your PR foundation. Paired with a keen understanding of the techniques that will help you garner positive attention for your brand, this combination is powerful in building brand recognition, earned media coverage and engagement.

But what does agility look like in public relations?

It could mean that you test out new social media tools as soon as they come out to find innovative ways to beat out your competitors. It could also mean modernizing the tried-and-true PR techniques you already use, like press releases, with things like videos and photos to attract more attention, or even trying out new software that streamlines your communications workflow.

Often, it requires a mix of platforms, tools, and strategies. The benefit of combining a solid foundation with agile strategies? Greater attention and interest from your audience, more earned media, and an increase in sales. So let's get back to those PR basics that you need in this digital age we live in.

We've broken out six areas you need to focus on, and provided detailed tips for each:

Press releases

Media and influencer lists

Pitching

Community engagement

Digital newsrooms

Measurement

How to Write a Press Release

Press releases have always been about boosting brand awareness via earned media coverage. That will never change; however, born from the digital revolution are new benchmarks, goals and strategies.

First of all, syndicating your press release to major news websites, industry publications and blogs will drive new and targeted traffic from audiences who wouldn't otherwise have ended up on your website. And using targeted keywords in your press release, especially your headline, can also help your release rise up in search results. Having your press release is published on Cison's industry-leading web properties, you are leveraging our digital authority, driving search visibility for your brand's keyword strategy. Ultimately, the majority of consumers trust earned media more than paid and owned content, and press releases play a vital role in how your target audience perceives your brand.

All that being said, it's important to craft a press release that journalists and people want to read. Here are a few tips.

Make it Newsworthy.

Always start by asking if the story is newsworthy. Writing a press release just to write one is a surefire way to get penalized by Google and ignored by consumers. Ask yourself: would this story be appropriate in the news section of the newspaper, or maybe a trade publication? Is it filled with facts or opinions? Does it tell a story or does it sound like an advertisement? Would your target audience want to read it? Press releases should always be about news.

Write an Engaging Headline.

Headlines are the first things, and often times the only things, people see, so take time to craft the best possible one. Google also crawls them, but usually only the first 70 characters, so keep yours short. Use statistics or numbers from your press release to engage readers.

Leverage Subheadings.

Google may or may not index the subheading and they don't appear in the newsrooms, but that doesn't mean it's wasted space. Use it to add context to your press release with important keywords and phrases. It also helps break up longer content to make it more readable.

Pique Interest in Your Introductory Paragraph.

Start with the lede. Don't bury it! Successful press releases present exciting information immediately rather than holding it back. Focus on answering who, what, when, where, why and how, at least at a high level. Then add detail in subsequent paragraphs.

Drive Audiences to Take Action.

Make sure to have a call-to-action in the release. The news release today is just as much for the end consumer as it is for a journalist. Direct the audience to take the action that you would like them to take. This should be included in the first 2-3 paragraphs. It should be clear, concise and compelling — bolded in the body of the press release.

Build It Out in the Body.

The body builds on that pertinent info you provided in the introduction. Add details, bullet points and quotes from key spokespeople to enhance your news. Don't give away everything here; the purpose of a press release isn't to provide a 1,000-word detailed account of your news, but rather to create curiosity, present the facts and motivate reporters, journalists, and consumers to get more information from you.

Leave Them Wanting More in the Conclusion.

The conclusion can be thought of as an "about" section or boilerplate. Share information about who your brand is and what it does. Wrap up with a restatement of why people should care about your news, and provide links where they can get more information about your brand.

Don't Forget the Contact Information!

Contact information — your business name, email, telephone number, website address, and social media handles — should always be up to date and easy to find in your press release. Press release distribution services sometimes place the details in a sidebar for easy access.

Add-In Visuals, Video, and Oth-

er Content.

This is your chance to stand out from the crowd. Multimedia features engage readers of your press release and make it stand out. Video, photos, audio clips, charts, and infographics provide additional meat to get people interested in your news. In fact, 71% journalists always or often use multimedia in the stories they write.

Creating and Maintaining Media and Influencer Lists

For press releases and other types of PR content to have the biggest impact, they should be shared with targeted media outlets and influencers. Identify the people who can best broadcast your message and put them on your media and influencer lists.
Finding journalists and influencers takes some work, but less than it did even just a few years ago. Today, media databases, website analytics, and audience demographics make it easier to find the right contacts for your message.

Use a Database.

Media databases and influencer discovery platforms, like the one provided by Cision, are a way to work smarter, not harder. Use databases to identify media outlets, influencers, and journalists — that not only cover your beat and vertical but influence your customers. Research those contacts so that you have a better idea of who they are, what they cover, and how best to pitch them.

Study Your Audience.

Need to find the top influencers for your audience? Study who your audience pays attention to. Who do they retweet regularly? What sites do they frequent? What content do they share? The Cision Media Database allows you to reverse engineer a search matching audience insights and demographics to influencers.
Use the answers to help you build a list of influencers that will pack the biggest punch with your target audience.

Keep Contact Information Up to Date.

Influencers come and go, as do journalists and reporters at a publication. Their topics of interest, beats, and outlets change, so it's important to update your influencer database regularly so

you always have the best point of contact. If it becomes too much of a hassle, most media databases have dedicated research teams to do your heavy lifting. Cision makes over 3 million database updates annually.

Time to Pitch Reporters, Journalists, and Influencers

Once you have your database of the media contacts you want to target your PR efforts to, it's time to pitch them.
Pitching is an art, and what works for reporters and journalists may not always work for influencers. Furthermore, what works for one reporter may not work for the next one.
According to Cision's 2017 Global Social Journalism Study, 90% of journalists use social media in their work, including finding topics to cover. Knowing this, you should use social media as well as email to reach the journalists, bloggers, and reporters you're targeting.
Because influencers are more of a mixed bag than journalists (some are YouTube sensations, while

Media people are like everybody else. If they don't find the information they want right away, they bounce. Make sure there's a link to your newsroom at the bottom of each page, or prominently displayed elsewhere. When you send journalists a link, send it directly to the newsroom so they don't have to hunt.

others attract crowds on social media), find out how they prefer to be pitched. Also remember that they're gatekeepers of a community, much more so than reporters. If you want to win their affection and attention, focus on how your story benefits their community rather than your brand.

Leverage Social Media to Build Rapport.

Social is the place for conversation. Find out what you have in common with reporters and influencers by paying attention to their social streams. Share their articles and congratulate them when they receive an award or other good news. Let them know when you hear news that's relevant to them. Make yourself a trusted, essential resource before pitching a story simply by showing up in their social media worlds.

Use Well-Structured Pitches.

Press release principles apply to your email pitches as well. Use a clear and enticing subject line, and keep the email copy to a minimum. If you've done your work well enough in warming up your contacts ahead of time, the reporter or influencer will already be interested in the story. Accompany the copy with links rather than attachments; files are often blocked by the recipient's firewall.

Track Your Efforts.

Always track whom you've pitched and what news or story idea you sent them. Also track who accepted the story and who didn't. If your first pitch doesn't succeed, try again with a different angle on the story, but only if the media contact is open to getting more pitches from you. Monitor the results and refine media lists and pitches accordingly.

How to Engage Your Community

If earned media received through your pitching or press release efforts makes up one arm of public relations, community management is another. You can have all the publicity in the world, but without brand advocates, it won't have

much reach. Those brand evangelists are, in fact, the ones who you want to hear your news and spread the word.
Social media has become a way to not only find breaking news stories and trends but also gauge audience reception and develop a loyal, engaged following. Your community will let you know what they want. Listen to what they're saying about you, and adjust your strategies and tactics accordingly.

Find Your Fans and Build a Community Around Them.

You want to reach your audience on the right social channels but realize: people use networks and apps that fit seamlessly into their lives and that provide value. Figure out which social sites fans spend their time on and develop a community on those channels.

Focus on Intrinsic, Not Extrinsic, Motivators.

People participate in communities when they enjoy the experience, find value, and feel they belong. If the community you create can do those things, people will stay, engage, and evangelize your brand.

Keep the Message Simple.

Think of this as an elevator pitch for your brand's community. Why should people join? What's in it for them? Maybe your cooking forum lets amateur chefs share tips and tricks. That's all it should do. Keep the purpose of your community streamlined so that fans will keep coming back, share it with their personal networks, and help grow the community.

Share Informative as Well as Fun Content.

The content you share depends on your brand and its goals. Certainly you occasionally want to provide information about your product, such as interesting ways to use it. But don't just focus on education and information; add in a few smile-inducing photos or articles to liven up your community. And get your audience involved! Maybe every week you feature one of your cooking community member's tip and share it on social media.

Repurpose Content for Each Channel.

While every piece of content should connect to a larger

narrative, the experience your community members have should be different on each channel. Messaging shouldn't be copied from Facebook to Snapchat to LinkedIn to Instagram, or else you will dilute the value of each. Learn the ins and outs of the channels, and use that information to guide how and what you share. Twitter is great for shorter messages (even though the 140-character count was recently expanded to 280 characters), while Instagram attracts photo-loving folks. Leverage what each social channel is good for and you'll see likes, comments, and word-of-mouth grow.

Ask People to Share Their Stories. Community is about people. Get participants involved by asking for stories and feedback. Encourage conversations by sharing and commenting on them to feed the fire.

By highlighting your most active community members, you not only show others that you get the thumbs up from your community, but you also make the members you shine the spotlight on that much more eager to support you.

Thank People for Their Involvement.

A little "thank you" can go a long way. Gratitude makes people feel appreciated and creates a sense of camaraderie. If you as a brand take the time to show your appreciation for community members talking up your brand, they'll gladly continue to do so and might even refer you business.

Track Your Efforts.

Social media efforts produce scads of data. In fact, it can be overwhelming just how much you can track. But determine your objectives first, then figure out which data will be the most useful. You might care more about the number of new followers you get each week, how many shares or likes you get, or how much traffic you drive to your website.
When you know the types of social updates, time of day, and images that get best results, you can modify your social media marketing accordingly.
And remember, social media is evolving. Keep an eye on rising networks and be ready to try them out if it makes sense for your brand.

Building a Digital

Newsroom

In the digital age, the term "newsroom" has been updated to reflect how businesses can show off their earned media mentions online.

The goal of a digital newsroom is to make marketing and PR content easy to find, access and use. Typically it consists of a page on a brand's website with links to articles, interviews, video clips, speaking events and any other media coverage a company has garnered along with key company facts.
This is the page you send reporters and influencers to when pitching them so that, should they want it, they can give additional information about your brand. Consumers, too, can access your online newsroom to learn more about your company.
Here, get tips on setting up your digital newsroom.

Figure Out What You Need to Include.

Especially if your PR team works overtime, you may have a plethora of media you could share on your digital newsroom page. Stick to the best and most relevant content to avoid inundating visitors with data.

Ask the Media What They Want.

Talk with the reporters and journalists you've built relationships with and ask them what they'd like to see in a digital newsroom. What's the most valuable? Beyond links to press releases and earned media, would they like access to logo or product images? The more aligned you are with what journalists want from your newsroom, the more value it will provide.
Make the Newsroom Easy to Find and Navigate.
Media people are like everybody else. If they don't find the information they want right away, they bounce. Make sure there's a link to your newsroom at the bottom of each page, or prominently displayed elsewhere. When you send journalists a link, send it directly to the newsroom so they don't have to hunt.
Always make links open to a new window for articles you house in your newsroom. You don't want people to navigate away from your website, so they can read the latest review of your product in a new tab, then come back to your site.

Provide Static and Dynamic Content.

Static content can include news releases, earned media clips, and awards announcements as well as blogs, white papers, and other owned content. Dynamic content refers to rich media, photo galleries, videos, graphics, and audio. A mix of the two will make your digital newsroom a success. As you get more media coverage, remove older links in favor of newer ones so that your media page isn't endlessly long.

List Contact Information.

Include contact details (email, phone, and social media) for your PR spokesperson on your newsroom page. Also consider creating a directory of company experts and key figures: people the media will want to interview.

Showcase Past and Upcoming Events.

Events are another way to establish your brand as a credible and authoritative voice in the marketplace, and including them on your media page can show that things are moving and shaking at your company. Plus, a detailed calendar can be the deciding factor in whether a reporter will give media coverage or seek you out at an event that they know you will be attending.

Analyze Your Efforts.

Ask the media for feedback. What's working and what isn't? Are there ways you can provide better value to a journalist who's strapped for time and needs to quickly locate the information she's seeking?
Also look at your analytics for the newsroom. How do your traffic numbers look? How are people interacting with content? Which features are getting clicked on the most?
Use feedback and analytics to improve the newsroom experience. Remember: your newsroom can and should be dynamic, so keep tweaking it for best results.

Measuring Your PR Efforts

Almost all the previous "basics" we've covered mention tracking or analyzing efforts, making this final point an obvious one: measure your work. Assessing results is critical, and there's really no

excuse not to. Data is plentiful and ready to be harvested.

Determine Your Objectives. Measurement only works if you know what you're trying to measure. What are the outcomes you hope to achieve? Look at both big picture and individual campaign goals

Once you've determined what you want to accomplish, write these goals down and share them with the team. Measurement works best when everyone's involvedand aimed toward the same target.

Monitor Results Along the Way. If you start with a benchmark of where things are before a given PR campaign, you can determine how much a given project moves the needle. Measure results after each and every campaign, and assess them alongside those benchmarks.

Analyze and Refine.

When something isn't working, change your approach. Do change only one thing at a time so that you know the factor that made the difference. And wait until a campaign is over before changing strategy; with public relations, it can sometimes take a while to get earned media mentions, so give them time to happen and spread your reach.

Repeat.

A PR pro's job is never done. Objectives change as the company matures or branches into other markets. New initiatives start. When they do, keep the principles of measurement in mind. They'll keep you on course and make sure you hit your target.

Keep Blending PR Basics with Innovation

The fundamentals of PR that we've covered here will always be ones you can rely on. They may look different as new technologies come and go, but they will never fail you. Adding in a bit of creativity and innovation as new tactics and tools come available will give you exactly what you and your stakeholders want: increased awareness, engagement, leads, sales, and loyalty.

SOURCE: PRWEB

IRRATIONALITY

A HISTORY OF THE DARK SIDE OF REASON

JUSTIN E. H. SMITH

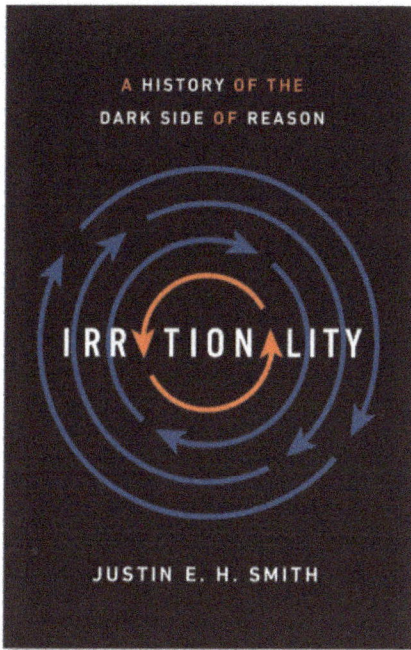

"A remarkable, erudite, and stylish book on an important and timely subject."
—Kieran Setiya, author of *Midlife: A Philosophical Guide*

Cloth $29.95

A LOT OF PEOPLE ARE SAYING

The New Conspiracism and the Assault on Democracy

RUSSELL MUIRHEAD AND NANCY L. ROSENBLUM

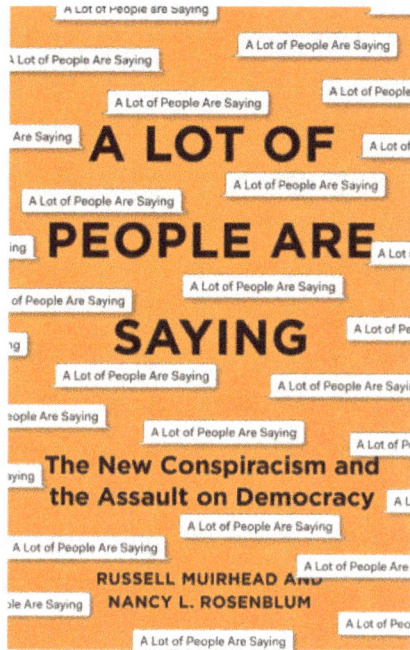

"The defining account of the stakes in the battle over misinformation and fake news in Western democracies."
—Brendan Nyhan, University of Michigan

Cloth $26.95

THE POWER OF CUTE

SIMON MAY

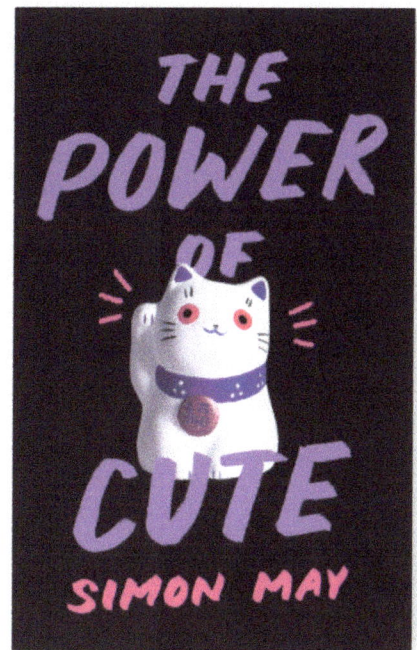

"Terrifyingly brilliant and continuously surprising."
—Jeffrey C. Alexander, Yale University

Cloth $18.95

DIGITAL RENAISSANCE

What Data and Economics Tell Us about the Future of Popular Culture

JOEL WALDFOGEL

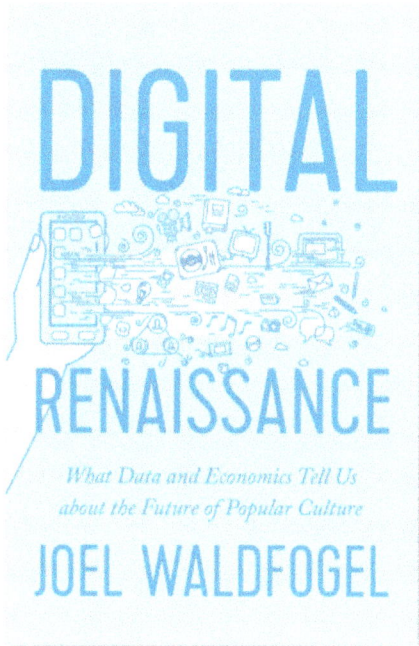

"A lucid, fascinating, and witty evidence-based account of how digital technology is transforming our cultural lives."
—Paul Seabright, author of *The Company of Strangers*

Cloth $27.95

THE WAR FOR GAUL

A NEW TRANSLATION

JULIUS CAESAR

TRANSLATED BY JAMES J. O'DONNELL

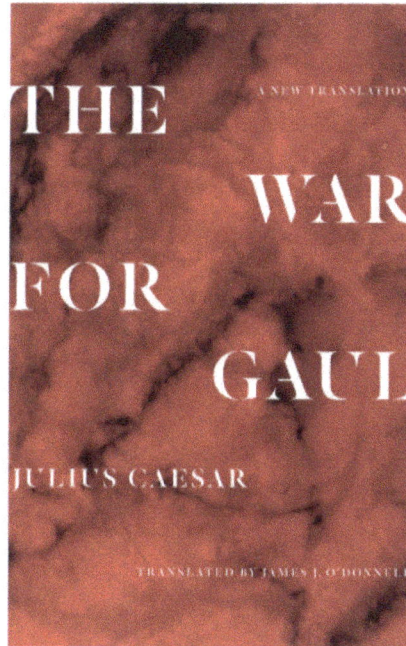

"James O'Donnell's version of *The War for Gaul* is as gripping and readable as Caesar's itself. Brisk, terse, and potent, the translation captures the meaning of the original. A marvelous achievement."
—Barry Strauss, author of *The Death of Caesar*

Cloth $27.95

UNEASY STREET

RACHEL SHERMAN

THE ANXIETIES OF AFFLUENCE

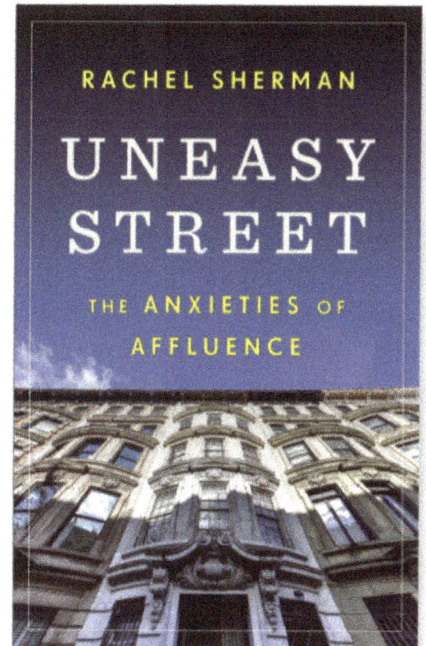

"Sherman offers something new and surprising: a look inside the 1 per cent's minds. . . . She shifts our understanding of today's dominant class."
—Simon Kuper, *Financial Times*

Paper $17.95

PRINCETON UNIVERSITY PRESS

GEORGE ELIOT 1819

Mary Ann Evans, who used the pen name George Eliot.

Mary Ann Evans (22 November 1819 – 22 December 1880; alternatively Mary Anne or Marian[1]), known by her pen name George Eliot, was an English novelist, poet, journalist, translator and one of the leading writers of the Victorian era. She wrote seven novels, Adam Bede (1859), The Mill on the Floss (1860), Silas Marner (1861), Romola (1862–63), Felix Holt, the Radical (1866), Middlemarch (1871–72) and Daniel Deronda (1876), most of which are set in provincial England and known for their realism and psychological insight.

Although female authors were published under their own names during her lifetime, she wanted to escape the stereotype of women's writing being limited to lighthearted romances. She also wanted to have her fiction judged separately from her already extensive and widely known work as an editor and critic. Another factor in her use of a pen name may have been a desire to shield her private life from public scrutiny, thus avoiding the scandal that would have arisen because of her relationship with the married George Henry Lewes.

Middlemarch has been described by the novelists Martin Amis[3] and Julian Barnes[4] as the greatest novel in the English language.

WORKS

NOVELS
Adam Bede, 1859
The Mill on the Floss, 1860
Silas Marner, 1861
Romola, 1863
Felix Holt, the Radical, 1866
Middlemarch, 1871–72
Daniel Deronda, 1876

POETRY
In a London Drawingroom, 1865
Two Lovers, 1866
The Choir Invisible, 1867
The Spanish Gypsy, 1868
Agatha, 1869
Brother and Sister, 1869
How Lisa Loved the King, 1869
Armgart, 1871
Stradivarius, 1873
The Legend of Jubal, 1874
I Grant You Ample Leave, 1874
Arion, 1874
A Minor Prophet, 1874
A College Breakfast Party, 1879
The Death of Moses, 1879
Count That Day Lost, 1887

https://iboo.com/en/george-eliot

George Eliot

DON'T LET CORPORATIONS PICK WHAT WEBSITES YOU VISIT

Broadband companies want the government to let them control the internet as we know it. And they've got help.

By Razan Azzarkani

Razan Azzarkani is a Next Leader at the Institute for Policy Studies. Distributed by OtherWords.org.

Think about the websites you visit. The movies you stream. The music you listen to online. The animal videos that are just too cute not to share.

Now think about the freedom to use the internet however and whenever you choose being taken away from you. That's exactly what Verizon, AT&T, Comcast, and other Internet Service Providers (ISPs), are trying to do.

Right now, those companies are constrained by a principle called net neutrality — the so-called "guiding principle of the internet." It's the idea that people should be free to access all the content available online without ISPs dictating how, when, and where that content can be accessed.

In other words, net neutrality holds that the company you pay for internet access can't control what you do online.

In 2015, the Federal Communications Commission adopted strong net neutrality rules that banned ISPs from slowing down connection speeds to competing services — e.g., Comcast can't slow down content or applications specific to Verizon because it wants you to switch to their services — or blocking websites in an effort to charge individuals or companies more for services they're already paying for. net-neutrality-internet

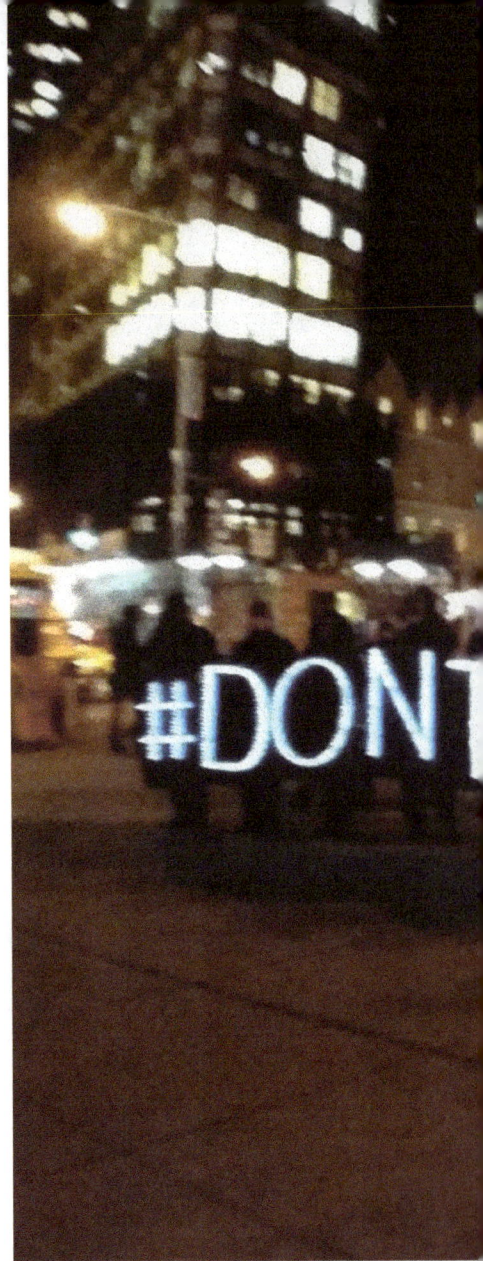

(Photo: Flickr/Backbone Campaign)

But now the open internet as we know it is under threat again.

Net neutrality rules are in danger of being overturned by Donald Trump's FCC chairman Ajit Pai and broadband companies like Comcast, AT&T, and Verizon.

But these corporations aren't doing this alone. They're getting help from at least eight handpicked members of Congress, all Republicans (Paul Ryan being the most notable), who've signed statements of support for overturning the neutrality rules.

(Photo: Flickr/Backbone Campaign)

Why? All we need to do is follow the money.

These eight lawmakers have all received significant campaign contributions from these corporations. That means the big broadband corporations and their special interest groups are attempting — and succeeding — to influence policymakers' decisions on rules that affect us all.

The fun doesn't stop there.

Ajit Pai — the FCC chairman bent on overturning net neutrality — is a former lawyer for Verizon, one of the very companies petitioning to have the rules changed. Lately Pai has been citing an academic paper arguing that the FCC "eschewed economics and embraced populism as [its] guiding principle" in making decisions on issues like net neutrality.

The catch? This paper wasn't written by independent experts. It was funded and commissioned by CA-Linnovates, a telecommunications industry trade group. Their biggest member? None other than AT&T, which stands to benefit a lot if these rules are overturned.

This is just one example of "information laundering," in which corporate-commissioned research is being used to further corporate agendas. It's just another way corporations are using their money and influence to lobby members of Congress. During a recent day of action, major websites such as Facebook, Twitter, and Google stood up in defense of net neutrality by using pop-up ads, GIFs, and videos to inform the public of the issue and ask them to tell the FCC to "preserve the open Internet."

You too can fight back against corporate influence by calling the FCC and telling them you won't give up your right to use the Internet the way you want.

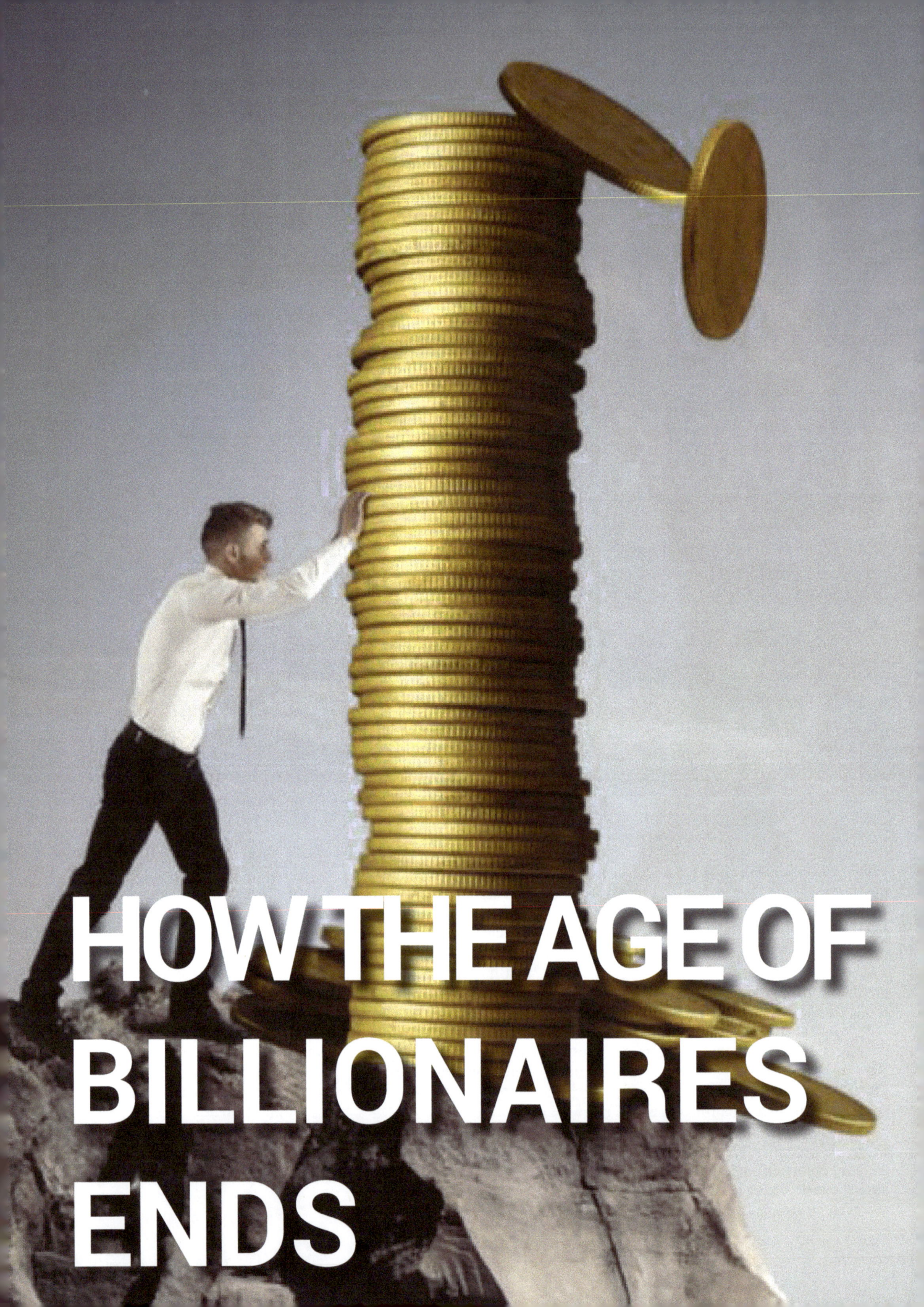

HOW THE AGE OF BILLIONAIRES ENDS

Serious proposals are on the table to address the deepening divide between the uber-rich and the rest of us.

By Josh Hoxie

Josh Hoxie directs the Project on Taxation and Opportunity at the Institute for Policy Studies. Distributed by OtherWords.org.

7 Every month or so there's a stunning new headline statistic about just how stark our economic divide has become. Understanding that this divide exists is a good start. Appreciating that a deeply unfair and unequal economy is problematic is even better. Actually doing something about it — that's the best.

As 2020 presidential hopefuls start trying to prove their progressive bona fides, serious policies to take on economic inequality are at the forefront. These ideas don't stand much of a shot of becoming law in the Trump era, of course. But if the balance of power shifts, so too does the potential for these paradigm-shifting new programs.

Let's take a closer look at the problems they'll have to address.

A new billionaire is minted every two days, according to a recent Oxfam study. As a result, the top 0.1 percent owns a greater share of the nation's wealth than the bottom 90 percent combined.

The richest dynastic families in the United States have seen their wealth expand at a dizzying pace. The three wealthiest families — the Waltons, the Kochs, and the Mars — increased their wealth by nearly 6,000 percent since 1983.

In other words, the rich in the United States have accumulated a metric crap ton of money. And what are they doing with this immense wealth and power?

Dan Snyder (#368 on the Forbes 400) just bought the world's first mega-yacht, with an IMAX theater on it, for $100 million. Hedge fund billionaire Kenneth Griffin (#45) just broke the record for the highest price ever paid for a house — $238 million — for an apartment in Manhattan's "Billionaires' Row."

Add in a few private jets, a couple of absurd presidential runs, and those Trump tax cuts, and you get a pretty accurate depiction of the priorities of billionaire spending.

Meanwhile, the rest of the country isn't shopping for yachts and jets. Most families are forced to work longer hours for lower wages. Despite massive increases in growth and productivity, the median family saw their wealth go down over the past three decades, not up. The proportion of families with zero or negative wealth (meaning they owe more than they own) jumped from 1 in 6 to 1 in 5.

Relatedly, our roads and bridges our crumbling and our public schools are desperately underfunded.

It doesn't take an economist to tell you this isn't sustainable. So what about those policies to do something about it?

Senator Bernie Sanders has proposed a robust addition to the federal estate tax. Billionaires under his plan would pay a top rate of 77 percent on whatever they bequeath to their heirs over $1 billion. (Far from a new idea, Sanders is merely proposing reinstating the top rate in place from 1941 to 1976.)

Senator Elizabeth Warren, not to be outdone, has proposed a direct tax on concentrated wealth targeting modern day wealth hoarders. Her plan would impose a progressive annual tax starting at 2 percent on assets over $50 million and rising to 3 percent on assets over $1 billion.

And at least one member of Congress who isn't running for president, Rep. Alexandria Ocasio-Cortez, has gotten in on the action. She's proposed raising the top marginal tax rate to 70 percent (only on income over $10 million, contrary to what you might hear on Fox News).

Three bold ideas to stem our skyrocketing economic inequality, three ways to tax the ultra-rich, three policies unlikely to become law given the current administration.

Yet these ideas are more than mere platitudes. Poll after poll shows big majorities of Americans ready to see the rich pay their fair share — and worried about the economic power consolidating in the upper echelons. When the political moment arrives, we won't have to wonder what's coming.

Correction: An earlier version of this op-ed incorrectly identified Dan Gilbert as the purchaser of the $100 billion yacht. It's been corrected to Dan Snyder.

How To Delete Your Data
FROM FACEBOOK FOREVER

To completely remove your Face-book profile and all the photos, videos, status updates and so on you've shared over the years, you'll need to permanently delete your Facebook account.

F acebook has agreed to pay a record $5 billion settle-ment to resolve an investigation into privacy viola-tions, the Federal Trade Commission (FTC) announced Wednesday. The company will also create an "inde-pendent privacy committee" to ensure "greater ac-countability at the board of directors level," an FTC press release says. But the settlement won't affect Facebook's corporate governance structure, which lets Zuckerberg hold sway over the company's actions.

Facebook has promised to clean up its act when it comes to privacy matters. But the social media giant's missteps have nonetheless cost it the trust of some users. 74% of adult Facebook users have either adjusted their privacy settings in the last year, taken a break from the site, or deleted the Face-book app from their phones, according to the Pew Research Center.

Of course, there are also more extreme measures you can take if you no longer trust Facebook — including deactivat-ing or deleting your Facebook account. Alternatively, you can review how much information you're sharing with and on the platform. Here's how to do all of those things.

How to permanently delete your Facebook account

To completely remove your Facebook profile and all the photos, videos, status updates and so on you've shared over the years, you'll need to permanently delete your Facebook account. Doing so will prevent you from using Facebook Messenger, as well as disable any Facebook-based logins you use for other services, like Spotify. (Facebook says you'll need to contact those sites to set up a new login.)

After deleting your Facebook account, you'll have a 30-

day window to change your mind. Once those 30 days are up, all your information will be permanently deleted and inaccessible. (Your information won't be viewable to other Facebook users during the 30-day period.) Facebook suggests users download their Facebook data—posts, photos, comments, and other profile information—before deleting an account. Facebook can create a password-protected file containing all your posts and other content that's downloadable a few days after being requested.

To permanently delete your Facebook account, navigate to the Setting page through the downward facing arrow at the top right side of the site. Click the Your Facebook Information link under Security and Login and navigate to the Delete Your Account and Information link. Once there, you'll have the option to Deactivate Account, which

Deactivate your Facebook account

There are other ways to take a step away from Facebook besides the nuclear option of fully deleting your account. Deactivating your Facebook account won't delete any of your data, but it will make your page inaccessible to other users. It might be a good option if you want to take a break from Facebook but don't want to go so far as deleting your account entirely. Deactivating your Facebook account will also allow you to continue using any Facebook logins and Facebook Messenger.

To deactivate your Facebook account, navigate to Settings through the downward-facing arrow on the top-right side of Facebook. Click Settings. Next, click on General and navigate to Manage your account. There you'll have the option to Deactivate your account.

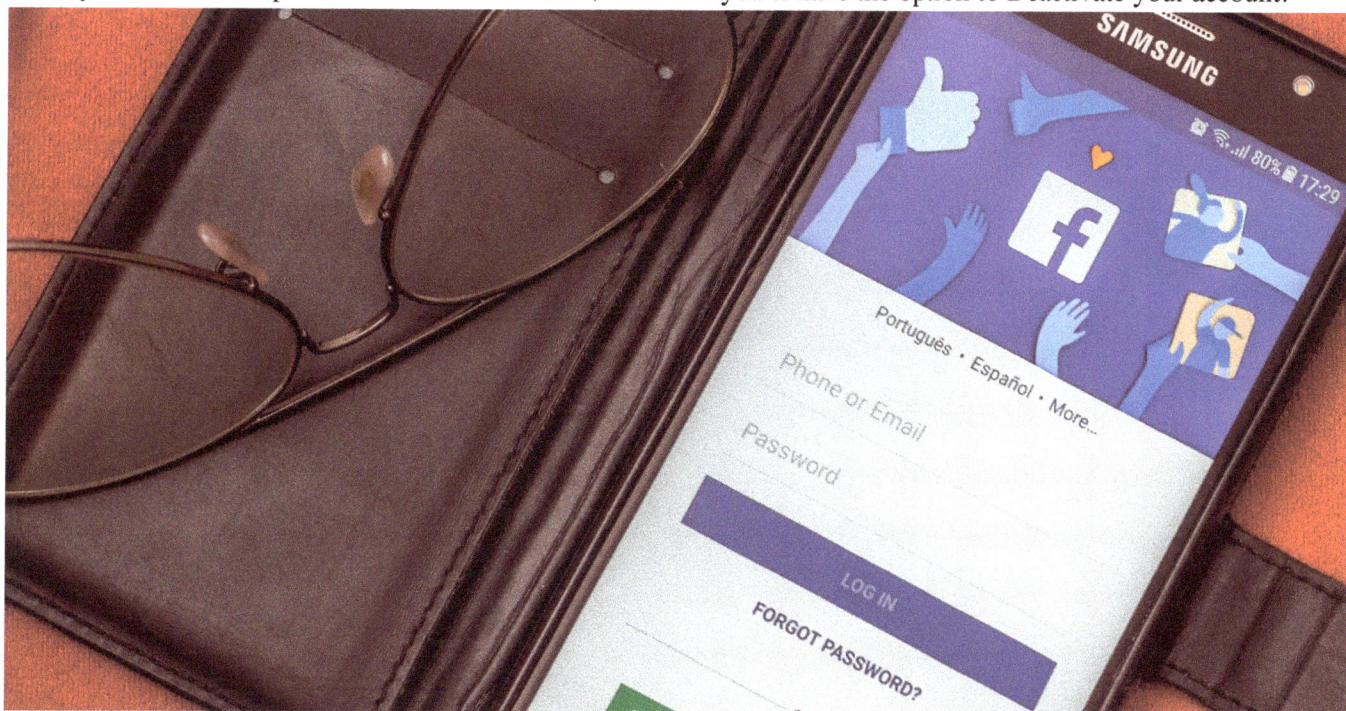

will allow you to either keep Messenger access, Download Your Information, or Delete Account.

Assuming you've already downloaded any data you want to keep, click Delete Account. You'll be prompted to enter your Facebook password. Click Continue and then Delete Your Account.

Again, you'll have 30 days to change your mind before all your Facebook data is permanently deleted. (To stop a deletion in progress, log into Facebook and you'll be prompted with the option to Cancel Deletion.) Facebook says that some information, "like messages you sent to friends," could still be visible to other users even after your account is deleted. Anything your friends have posted about you will also remain on Facebook, since that's their data and not yours.

Manually delete information

Depending on your privacy settings, everything you've ever posted to Facebook, as well as anything you've been tagged in, may be viewable on Facebook's Your Information page. Your data is separated into different categories, including posts, photos, likes and more. This is handy if you don't want to delete all your Facebook data, but simply want to scroll through your user history and curate what your Facebook page displays.

You can also manually delete your information on this page — but it will likely be a time-consuming process if you've been on Facebook for a while.

www.ingramcontent.com/pod-product-compliance
Lightning Source LLC
Chambersburg PA
CBHW052348210326
41597CB00037B/6295